# ✝FREED
## by His Love

### A CATHOLIC WOMAN'S JOURNEY TO
### SPIRITUAL AND PHYSICAL HEALING

By Cheryle Miller

☧

☧

# Contents

☧

# Foreward

"One Prays for Miracles, but works for results." ~Saint Augustine
I have known Cheryle Miller for more than eight years as her pastor.
The Miller family had been very active in parish activities, whether
it be spiritual or social events and Cheryle, along with some other
parishioners, had been instrumental in bringing 24-hour adoration
to the parish.

I remember Cheryle telling me about her health; that she was diagnosed with Trigeminal Neuralgia. As days went by and things got
worse, Cheryle remained hopeful and trusted in the Lord even at the
worst moments. In these moments, we had many conversations on
perseverance through God.

When I heard that Cheryle was healed, my first thought was to wait
to be sure, but when it was confirmed again and again that she was
healed, I was reminded that miracles still happen! As I am reminded
of the many conversations Cheryle and I had, it is still difficult for me
to comprehend this miracle of healing!

When I read the book, Freed by His Love, I was moved to thank God
for what He had done to bring hope to this hopeless situation and
I was reminded that God is closer and more active than I had ever
imagined! This book is an inspiration, giving strength and hope to
anyone who is struggling in life. Whether it be health, finances, relationships, or any other physical or spiritual difficulty, I hope Cheryle's
story reminds people that all one needs is to trust in the Lord and to
call upon His name.

Thank you, Cheryle, for this inspiration and for never giving up on
the miracle God had in store for you.

Fr. Jacob Dio, MSFS
(Pastor)
Immaculate Conception Catholic Church

�֍

# CHAPTER 1: THE BEGINNING
## 1968–1997

*"No one can come to me unless the Father who sent me draw him, and I will raise him on the last day." —John 6:44*

I was five years old and so excited to start kindergarten in the Catholic school that was right across the street from my house. I was even more excited to find out that my kindergarten teacher was going to be my aunt. There was no need to shop for school clothes because we wore uniforms. The skirt was gray plaid with pleats, the top a crisp, white blouse with the option of a sweater or vest over it.

I remember my first day well. I went to my classroom and there was my aunt. She was so sweet. My desk was right up front. As children arrived, my aunt greeted them and told them to find their seats. She then went to the blackboard and wrote her name. "My name is Mrs. Lippold, but Cheryle can call me Aunt Edna." I turned red because I never expected her to say that. The girl next to me turned and said, "Well, aren't you special." My elation of starting school deflated like a popped balloon.

To make matters worse, the principal walked into the classroom. Sister Ignatius was in her fifties and wore a formal habit. She didn't smile very often, but I understood that to mean she took her job as principal seriously. She was walking down the aisle and when she got to me, she stopped. "Young lady." My aunt gave her my name and said that I was her niece. She frowned at my aunt. "There will be no favoritism, Mrs. Lippold." I had a lump in my throat like I'd swallowed a big pill without water.

The excitement of school was gone forever after that day. I was not only the constant entertainment of bullies, but the nuns were not very encouraging. During uniform inspection, Sister Ignatius would make us kneel to see if our uniform skirts touched the floor. If it was too short, the girl would be sent home. I trembled when she walked in the classroom, even though my uniform was the proper length, because Sister would always find something wrong with me. I had very long hair that she seemed to despise. Every time we had one of those "take a knee" drills, I would end up with a rubber band in my hair. Once or twice a week, my mom would have to cut the rubber band out of my hair along with the hair entangled in it.

The bullying continued throughout my time in grade school. Every year, the sixth-grade class would have a live Nativity scene at the end of the Christmas play. I used to dream about the time when I would be in sixth grade. I hoped that maybe I would get the part of Mary.

When I was finally in sixth grade, as Christmas drew closer, the only thing I thought about was who would play the part of Mary. One day in December, my teacher made an announcement. "This year, the part of Mary in the Nativity scene will go to . . . Cheryle. What! Had I heard correctly? I got the part! I was so excited!

Shortly after that day, my friends and I were eating lunch together, and they asked me to go to the bathroom with them. This wasn't out of the ordinary because girls always go to the bathroom together. When I walked through the bathroom door, all the girls in my class were standing there. I had no idea why. All of a sudden, one of the girls grabbed my arms and put them behind me and one by one, each girl, even girls I thought were my friends, punched me in the stomach, in the face, and pulled out handfuls of hair. I didn't fight back. I don't even remember what I did.

One of the popular girls finally spoke up. "That part was for me."

Needless to say, when my teacher and parents saw what I looked like, all the girls were reprimanded. I stayed home from school for a couple of days to recoup. I was afraid to go back.

Despite the way those girls treated me, when it was time for the play, I was still so excited. When I was on that stage, even though I was holding a plastic doll in my hands, something supernatural happened to me. I was so happy. I didn't really have a devotion to Mary at the time, but I knew that she was the Mother of God. It was as if I could sense the love that she had for Jesus.

Because I didn't fight back, the Devil used this to tell me how weak I was. This incident actually hardened my heart and changed my personality. Soon after that bathroom incident, I started to dress inappropriately, become flirtatious, and desired to fit in no matter the cost. Years later, when I pondered on Jesus' Passion, I noticed that He never fought back, either. He turned the other cheek. Jesus eventually healed this deep wound that I had carried around for many years.

––––––––––

In this environment, if we misbehaved, the nuns would say, "You are going to go to hell." These were good women, I believe. They were just doing what they'd been taught, even if their approach was not very good. I grew up with a fear of God and a bit of scrupulosity. I didn't understand what that was at the time, I just wanted to be perfect so I wouldn't be picked on so much. A merciful, loving God was never talked about. But as time went on, that fear I felt of God eventually melted away.

I was blessed with very faithful Catholic grandmas on both my mother and father's sides. In their own ways, they presented God's love to me. My father's mom used to go to daily Mass and wore a beautiful black veil. She was a widow. I never knew my grandpa except through photographs. My dad looked a lot like him.

My maternal grandma, my mom, and my aunt were involved in the charismatic movement in the early eighties, which was right around the time that I met Jon. I went to prayer meetings with them, but I was not open to that form of praise and worship. I was so caught up in perfectionism and scrupulosity that I didn't know how to just relax. I was intrigued and kept going, but I found myself holding back, keeping God at a distance. The priest that ran these prayer groups was one of my high school teachers. He is the priest that Jon and I asked to marry us. I was twenty-three and Jon was twenty-two.

We had a beautiful, Catholic wedding. Not knowing my faith at the time, we picked the date randomly. We met in November of 1981, dated for eleven months, were engaged for eleven months, and got married on October 1. Eleven seemed to be our "lucky" number. Years after, I found out that St. Therese of Lisieux's feast day is our anniversary date. It seems God had a plan that I was not aware of at the time.

Jon was raised Catholic by his father. His mother was Lutheran. Jon's father and his seven siblings went to Mass every Sunday. I am thankful that my father-in-law made the effort to ensure that his children went to church and made their sacraments. Jon was an altar server. Despite the little formation he received about his Catholic faith, he never left the church. He kept going to Sunday Mass even after he graduated high school. Looking back, we both think he stayed because of the time he served on the altar. He said that the first time he served at Mass, he wanted to stay and serve for all of the Masses. He often tears up when he sees our grandson, Jadin, serve at Mass.

---

Fast forward to the year 1992. Jon and I had just built a new home down the road from my parents' house. Most of our extended family lived within thirty minutes of us. We were centrally located and so happy to be around our family. We were trying to move in prior to the birth of our third daughter, Rachel. By this time, we had Melissa who was seven, Laura was six, and soon to join us was Rachel. As I was getting settled into the house, instead of having a peaceful feeling, something didn't seem right. I had this gnawing feeling in the pit of my stomach that soon things would change again.

Not understanding how these feelings can be from the Holy Spirit, I kept hearing in my heart that we should move out of state. I pushed the idea aside, thinking it was just nonsense. I didn't understand that God actually communicates with people in many ways.

Life kept marching on with the birth of our fourth daughter, Emily, in 1994. I was busy working part time as the town clerk of the little town we lived in. Raising four children was my main job. But the cymbals in my head to move kept getting louder, despite my busy life.

One night, after putting our four girls to bed, I spoke to Jon about the idea of moving out of state. Jon and I had mentioned it many times before, but we never took it any further. Jon looked at me, surprised. He needed a few days to think about it. We had very different personalities at the time. Over the years, the Lord has tamed me. I was the type of person who would take a task and run with it. When given an assignment in class, even if it wasn't due for two weeks, I would rush home and start working on it right away. I was the opposite of procrastination, but it still was not the healthiest approach. Jon, on the other hand, took his time making up his mind and thought things through completely.

A few weeks later, we decided to roll the dice and look at jobs elsewhere. Jon's job was as a loose-leaf binder set-up person. We had no clue this type of job was such a specialty. Jon is also an amazing woodworker. In New York, woodworking was not a promising career path as there were no jobs in this field in the area.

We did research to see which states would have woodworking careers. We also wanted to move to a state without snow. After getting up a half hour early every day in the winter to snow blow the 250-foot driveway just to get to work, Jon and I both wanted to move to warmer weather. We sent his resume to jobs in Tennessee and Kentucky. He received three offers, two in Tennessee and one in Kentucky. We decided on Tennessee because we have relatives in Greeneville, Tennessee. We didn't have a clue that God was leading us right where He wanted us.

On June 20, 1998, which happened to be Jon's birthday, we moved to Middle Tennessee from Western New York. Our move was less than perfect. We managed to fit everything that we owned from fifteen years of marriage into a rented moving truck.

The moving truck's air conditioning was broken. Jon rode in the truck with our dog, Princess, a mixed breed of German Shepherd and Greyhound. We'd had her since she was a puppy. Unfortunately, she could keep up with every car that came down our very rural road in New York. Her sense of smell was amazing. We used to test it out by having one of our girls take a certain path and hide. We would then command Princess to go find her. Using that keen nose of hers, she was able to follow the exact path to where my daughter hid.

She was a sensitive dog. Every time she got stressed, she would shed. Riding in a moving van across many states, it wasn't surprising that she started to shed intensely. My poor husband was sweating in the truck with a shedding dog. When we stopped, he looked like he was tarred and feathered.

I drove the family van with the four girls. At one point, we were stopped in traffic just next to an exit. I started to move and then pushed the brake, but nothing happened. I stomped on the brake harder. Thankfully, I was going slow enough that the van stopped. I pulled off on that exit. God, in His mercy, provided for us because we just happened to be at the only exit in the area that had a twenty-four-hour truck stop mechanic shop. The mechanic agreed to fix our brake line for only $40. What a saintly man. Right next to the truck stop was a hotel, so we stayed the night there and left again the next morning.

When we arrived in Tennessee, we had to stay in an extended stay hotel until we closed on our house. Since no pets were allowed, we had to board our dog. The boarding kennel had very low fences. I warned them that our dog was part greyhound and could jump that fence easily. Two days later, we came to visit our dog. We pulled into the driveway and the owner ran out of the house frantically. She said, "Your dog just jumped the fence and we can't find her." The mood in the car changed from laughing to four girls crying hysterically.

Jon jumped out of the car and started calling to her. She had gotten loose in New York before but always found her way home, but she was unfamiliar with this new place. For weeks, we would try to find her, walking the streets and asking people in the area. We checked with the dog pounds so frequently that they recognized our voices. I guess it was easy for them to remember since we had New York accents. We never found her. We lost a member of our family that day.

The Devil was trying really hard to foil our move. Jon and I took that as confirmation that we'd made the right choice. As the years went by, we all agreed that moving to Tennessee was the best choice for our family. This was the first time that I remember hearing and obeying God.

# Chapter 2: Deeper Steps of Faith
## 1998–2007

*"[Jesus] said to them, 'Because of your little faith. Amen, I say to you, if you have faith the size of a mustard seed, you will say to this mountain, "Move from here to there," and it will move. Nothing will be impossible for you."* —Matthew 17:20

We, as lukewarm Catholics, found ourselves in the Bible Belt. It was the first time that we saw people actually living their faith. God knew that I needed a strong spiritual influence so He didn't waste any time in allowing me to meet Mary.

Mary, my spiritual sister, has helped grow my faith in ways that I never imagined. God used her to aid me along this path. Little did I know, God was taking me on a journey of love.

Our family registered with the Catholic Church in our town. We were surprised at the welcome we received. There was something beautiful about the church and the people there. Their faith in God was evident and powerful. I slowly started to gravitate toward them.

My friend, Mary, was homeschooling her children and so I met many other homeschooling moms who were also very faithful. I sometimes felt like I didn't fit in because I was still thinking in ways that were contrary to the church's teachings. I was not aware of my errors.

After we settled into life in Tennessee, I decided that when Emily started school that I would go to work. I have always worked around the family, mostly part time, but this would be the first time that I would venture into a full-time career. I had mixed emotions because I always loved being the mom who would show up at school to have lunch with her child. I was the mother who would go on field trips, plays, concerts, birthday parties at school, you name it, I was there. I fell into a worldly happiness. Two family income with two cars, a big house—the American Dream. I ventured into a career growth that really stunted my spiritual growth, but God had other plans.

It was the year 2000; we survived the Y2K scare. I had just begun working when my oldest daughter, Melissa, started to have grand mal seizures. The first time this happened, I was talking on the phone to her. All of a sudden, the phone dropped and I could hear my younger daughters panicking. I was terrified. Jon and I had never seen an epileptic person before, so we thought that she was dying. It took us many visits to her neurologist and a week in the hospital to finally find the right medication for her. She still would have break-through seizures. She is thirty-five years old now and will be on medication the rest of her life.

This was the first time that I had to face the reality that I could not protect my children. I had no control over anything. I remember going outside early in the morning on a few occasions just crying to God about my daughter. Why did this have to happen to her?

Through this experience, God taught me that He was in charge and I was not. For years, I felt so much stress and weight on my shoulders to make the right decisions. Jon and I never prayed about anything. We just did what we thought was right. What I didn't understand was that God was with me this whole time. Looking back, I have to apologize to Jesus for not trusting in Him, not knowing that He is Mercy and Love. I thought Jon and I had to make these decisions even though I was never certain of the outcome.

In the meantime, I was growing closer to my church friends. They taught me a lot about my faith that I didn't know. I wanted to learn more, but instead, I decided to grow my career in technology. God, in His mercy, allowed me to reach the so-called dreams I had on the career path I had chosen. It wasn't because He wanted me on that path, but because He was showing me that there was no happiness in this direction. This lesson took me about four years to learn.

The last job that I took outside of the house involved me traveling. I was gone for weeks at a time and my family seemed to start falling apart. My oldest became very rebellious because of not dealing well with her illness. My youngest was diagnosed with migraines, and Jon was miserable without me.

Every day that I drove to work, I listened to contemporary Christian music. My commute was about forty minutes. I used this time to pray, and I kept saying to God that I needed a change. I couldn't leave my family again.

The last work trip, I was gone for a full week. I remember being all dressed up and waiting to board the plane. Everyone around me was busy looking at notes, their computers, or their phone. I just looked out the window and tears welled up inside me. I looked like I had it all together, but inside I was a mess.

I knew that God was telling me that I had to let go of this part of my life. I had another work trip coming up, and I just couldn't do it. My younger daughters were having trouble in school. My friends at church encouraged me to consider homeschooling Rachel and Emily.

I was praying to God, asking Him what He wanted me to do, and I kept hearing the song, "Dive" by Stephen Curtis Chapman on my commute to the office. The song is about taking a leap of faith. In other words, trusting in God and making a change.

One day, not long after that, I talked things over with my husband. The next day, I walked into my boss's office. "I have to quit," I said. My boss was very understanding and asked me to stay on, but I said, "No, I just can't be away from my family anymore." I took the leap of faith.

At first, we were in a panic because I had been making more money than Jon. Despite that, the peace that I had from this decision was immediate and we made some financial adjustments to accommodate for this change. Suddenly, I was awakened by the fact that God, and not the world, was truly guiding me. The peace that flowed through my veins was like a small waterfall gushing into the dead areas in my body that needed God's Living Water.

Once, I had a dream about a house. In the dream, I walked from room to room. I opened the door to this one room and inside were dead plants everywhere. God used this analogy because I love growing houseplants. Jon was with me in this dream, and I asked him what he thought had happened in this room. I prayed about this dream for a long time and God finally revealed to me that this was my heart. I was not giving it life. I was good at the temporal things, but the spiritual, not so good. He is the way, the truth and the life. Living like I believed this brought forth new life in me. My heart felt alive again. I now picture my heart full of so many flowers and plants of all kinds, giving an aroma of joy and love to everyone around me.

I was so happy being home. That's when God put it on my heart to homeschool my girls. My older two daughters had already graduated by then; there is a nine-year difference between the oldest and youngest. I took Rachel and Emily out of school when they were in fourth and fifth grades. I was worried that I wouldn't teach them well enough. The first year was a struggle. By the second year, I started to get the hang of it. I also noticed that my daughters were much happier.

When I started to teach the girls about their Catholic faith, I learned too. Our faith and its richness came alive for me. I also took the children to daily Mass. I grew more in love with Jesus through Mass, which is the highest form of worship to God. Receiving Jesus body and blood every day is an amazing gift from Him.

*"As the living Father sent me, and I live because of the Father, so whoever feeds on me, he also will live because of me" (John 6:57, ESV).*

# Chapter 3: The Diagnosis
## 2008–2014

*"Give ear to my words, O Lord; understand my sighing. Attend to the sound of my cry, my king and my God!"*
*—Psalm 5:2–3*

I loved the time that I could be home with my children, but I did take another job. I was very fortunate to be able to work from home full time so that we could have insurance for our children. Jon is an amazing woodworker, but, unfortunately, his job didn't provide medical insurance. My daughter Laura and I worked at the same company from home as sales associates. Since the company was open twenty-four hours, I was able to switch my schedule to an early-morning shift to accommodate homeschooling my girls.

Unfortunately, during that time, I was not able to go to daily Mass except on my days off. My hunger for God in His Eucharistic form grew and grew. I also knew that my vocation as wife and mother were very important. I accepted that this was what my life would be like for a time. I learned that even the most menial tasks, if offered up to God with love, were great gifts to Him. Instead of complaining so much about my tasks, I learned to accept them.

When I started to do this, everything I did seemed better. My family complimented me on the meals I made. I was able to clean the house and all of my other duties with happiness. My daughter makes fun of me because I used to make a list of my chores. After each one was done, I would say, "Another one bites the dust!"

While home, I learned more prayers and read the Bible and other spiritual books. Despite my longing for Mass, Jesus filled me in other ways.

During this time, I noticed I was getting headaches. Also, my teeth would hurt. I made frequent trips to the dentist. I switched dentists, too, because I had such pain in my teeth, and I felt like nobody would help me. I begged them to just pull my teeth. It's not normal that you would beg your dentist to pull your teeth out, but I just couldn't deal with the pain. I had a few cracked teeth so my new dentist thought they were the culprit. The pain would lessen for a few months, but then it would flare up again. The headaches would make putting the headset I wore during work painful.

It was 2011, my two youngest daughters graduated high school, and I was done with homeschooling. I switched my schedule so that I could attend daily Mass more often. I was so happy to be able to come back to church on a daily basis. I think that the Lord was preparing me for what was to come.

I was promoted to Call Center Supervisor in August 2013. I had to start working third shift. After working an early morning shift for so many years, it was a great shock to my system. The headaches started to get worse and no pain killers would lessen the severity. I thought I just needed a break from work. So Jon and I planned a vacation.

On October 1, 2013, we celebrated our thirtieth anniversary with a trip to Venice Beach in Florida to hunt for shark teeth. I found the largest one, despite Jon's vigorous searches. We laughed and had a good time, but I noticed something unusual. The wind off the ocean was strong and although it was warm, it caused my head to hurt. I didn't think anything of it until the next day when the headache returned. Mind you, I had been having headaches and tooth aches for about two years at that point.

When we returned from our trip, I was busy with work and holiday preparations, but on January 14, 2014, I finally went back to my dentist. I was complaining again about a tooth that was giving me pain. After looking at x-rays and seeing there was nothing, he was perplexed. He didn't know what to think but said he was going to do some research first. On my way home, he called me and said, "Cheryle,

I think that you have Trigeminal Neuralgia." I'd never heard of this. "What is that?" I asked. He told me to look it up when I got home and referred me to a neurologist.

When I got home, I looked it up and was shocked. Suddenly, seeing the words in front of me made perfect sense. I had many of the symptoms. At that time, the pain was not constant, and for that I felt a sense of relief. But I also felt uncertain about what would happen next. When you find out the illness you have is nicknamed the Suicide Disease, it makes you nervous.

Thankfully, we had a family neurologist that I could trust (due to my daughter having epilepsy), so I went to see him. He listened to me describe my symptoms. He agreed with my dentist. After ordering tests which included an MRI, he started me on anti-convulsant (epilepsy) medicine. The first time I took the medicine trial, it alleviated the pain, which told the neurologist that we were definitely on the right track. This was the beginning of my seven-year ordeal with what I referred to as "the beast."

The medication trial didn't last long, and soon I was up to the highest dose and it wasn't helping at all. So my neurologist switched me to another medication and then another. Either I had reactions to them or they just didn't work. I felt like a lab rat being experimented with. This cycle continued for about a year. Finally, the medication Trileptal, the generic name is oxcarbazepine, seemed to help.

As the months passed, in spite of the medicine, I steadily grew worse. I had every symptom and some different ones too. I was so scared. How was I supposed to handle pain so severe that people kill themselves over it?

# Chapter 4: My Life Changed

*"Out of the depths I call to you, Lord; Lord, hear my cry! May your ears be attentive to my cry for mercy."* —Psalm 130:1–2

I was asked to write a narrative of how my life changed after being diagnosed with Trigeminal Neuralgia. I am including excerpts of my original answer because it explains the gravity of my illness and the despair I felt. I still wasn't at the place where I trusted God enough. Here is my answer:

———————

I was diagnosed with Trigeminal Neuralgia when I was fifty-two years old. I was a very active woman always gardening, working outside, walking and exercising, and watching my grandchildren. I was active in my church and had a very responsible Call Center Supervisor job from which I just recently resigned. The following is a description of my life.

I can no longer walk outside unless I am totally covered up with some kind of protection because the sun and wind (and just the slightest breeze) cause unspeakable face pain. I have a handicapped sticker so that I can park close to the door. Even if I am covered and go outside for more than five minutes, this is what happens to me:

My face feels like someone just poured hot coals on it. My nose feels like someone punched me. My lips feel burned. My left ear feels like it is infected. I have trouble hearing because it feels like it is full of water. My eyes hurt so bad, as if someone is trying to poke them out with a stick. They are under so much pressure that they feel like they are going to pop out of my head. I cannot even touch the top of my head or hair without major pain.

All of this is from just going outside! In addition to this, my face burns all the time. The pain never goes away. When I brush my teeth, my gums and teeth feel like I just had ten teeth pulled.

The medicine only takes the edge off. I do not have a good quality of life. I spend my whole day just making sure to avoid the things that cause me pain.

I have to stay inside in a controlled environment. I cannot be near the air conditioning vent or have a fan blowing on me. I have this controlled in my house but, of course, I do not have that luxury outside of my home. Can you imagine going shopping and having to watch where all the fans or air conditioning vents are? That is me.

I no longer have the freedom I used to. I can no longer do anything outside. Can you imagine not walking to the mailbox to get the mail? Not being able to watch your grandson play baseball? Not being able to go to any outdoor event?

The medicine I am on makes me very tired. I can only accomplish making dinner and possibly doing some laundry. That's on a good day. Most of the time, I am just barely getting off the couch. I cannot do the things I used to do. I have had to give up all of my extra-curricular activities in church and elsewhere. The medicine and lack of exercise have affected my weight.

I'm depressed for what I have lost. It's almost a mourning. There is no cure, only pain management, and from what I hear from support groups, the medicines only work for a short time and then either I'll have to increase the dosage or try another drug. The other option is brain surgery, which has a low success rate, which I might have to consider given the level of pain I'm in and no cure in sight.

I cannot ride in a car for more than an hour because the bouncing from the car causes so much pain.

This is a very lonely life.

I have to fight to even do the small things.

I used to take for granted taking a shower, brushing my teeth, brushing my hair, putting makeup on. All of these activities hurt so much. There is no cure. There is no end in sight. This is my life forever.

The Trileptal medication that I am on has reached the toxic level and no other medication seems to help. This is a chronic illness. I hate to hear, "I hope you get better soon." I will NEVER get better soon. I just have to manage my pain.

---

From my description, it's obvious just how extreme the pain level and despair was. I had no hope. You don't realize the things that you can't do because of pain. On a bad day, I couldn't even take the top off of my water bottle. I couldn't vacuum, cut vegetables, or pick up heavy objects. The pressure on my head was just so great.

In my despair and dismay at the radical changes in my life, I forgot to turn to God. I just kept praying out of despair for healing.

I didn't handle this change very well. I was crying all the time, which made the pain worse. Instead of putting Christ in the center, I was putting my needs in the center. The more that I paid attention to my pain, the more it ruled me.

## TRIGEMINAL NEURALGIA

The Trigeminal nerve runs along your face to give sensation, so when, for instance, you rub your nose because you have an itch, or you have food on your lip, or you have a tooth ache, you feel it. This nerve controls the feelings on your whole face. There is a Trigeminal nerve on either side of your face.

When the nerve is damaged, the slightest touch to your face sends out improper signals and instead of acting normal, the nerve works overtime. So, just like an electric cord that is stripped of its coating sends out shocks and sparks, a damaged Trigeminal nerve does the same.

A person may start out with short, mild attacks, but it can progress to longer attacks, and it eventually can become a continual pain. It occurs in women more than men and people over fifty. I was fifty-two when I was diagnosed.

Trigeminal Neuralgia symptoms are: severe shooting pains that

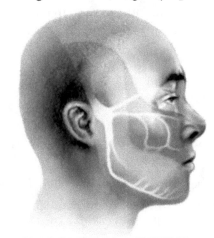 are shock-like. Sudden pain triggered by things such as touching the face, chewing, speaking, or brushing your teeth. Shooting pain can last a few seconds to a few minutes. Constant aching or a burning feeling may occur before it evolves into the spasm-like pain. The Trigeminal nerve gives feeling to the areas of the cheeks, jaw, teeth, gums, lips, eyes and forehead.

When the nerve is damaged, it becomes over-sensitive and causes extreme pain with shock-like movements in some or all of these areas. I was unfortunate and had the whole left side of the face and even my ear react to pain.

I received shocks like an electric current going through my face at my slightest movement, including speaking. The pain was constant like a rock was being pushed down into my head.

I loved to walk outside and have a warm, gentle breeze brush against my face. It reminded me how the Holy Spirit was like the wind, the breath of life. These things: the wind, the air conditioning, the slight breeze when someone walks by you, the steam that comes up from a hot cup of soup, the heat that comes when you open the door of your home and feel the welcomed warmth on a cold day . . . All of this gave me the most excruciating pain that I have ever felt.

God was with me all the time because He allowed me to find a Facebook support group that helped me deal with this new diagnosis. The members kept talking about MVD. I finally asked what it was and learned it is brain surgery called Microvascular Decompression. The surgeon cuts a round circle, literally with a hole saw, into your skull and, with major magnifying lenses on, operates on a very tiny portion of the trigeminal nerve. He looks for blood vessels that could be rubbing against the nerve, wearing away the protective myelin sheath. Like an electrical cord when the coating wears off, the cord shocks. This is what was happening to me. Shocks would come out of nowhere and you could see my head jump despite how hard I tried to hide it. I had no control over it.

There are very few doctors who could do this type of surgery and God came through, as always, because there was a specialist in Nashville who had performed many of these surgeries. People come to him from all over the world. He did at least two hundred of these surgeries every year. His name is Dr. Robert Mericle. With a last name like that, I knew I was in good hands. He was confident that he could help me. I met with him on August 2, 2014. I was aware that these surgeries had a 50/50 chance of failing, but with the amount of pain I was in, I didn't hesitate. The surgery was scheduled for September 16.

The day of the surgery couldn't arrive soon enough. Jon, Emily, and I rode the forty-five-minute trip to Southern Hills Hospital in complete silence. My mind was racing. What if I didn't wake up? I already received the Anointing of the Sick and made a good Confession, so I was spiritually prepared. I didn't think that Jesus was ready to take me yet, though.

What was I doing having brain surgery? Hitting a bump in the road on the way to the hospital reminded me why I was doing this. I wasn't concerned about the healing time, I just wanted it take away my pain. If the pain wasn't so riveting, I would have never in a million years considered someone operating on my brain! This, in itself, proves the gravity of my pain and my complete desperation.

When we arrived at the hospital, I was brought back into a room to prepare for surgery. The nurses had to put a line in for intravenous fluids. The surgery would last seven or eight hours.

My family was allowed to come back to the room. Jon and the girls walked in, except Rachel had to work. Just then my phone rang. Jon answered it. "It's Rachel." I picked up the phone and could hear her crying. "Mom, I really want to be there, but I have to work and can't get out of it." I told her not to worry. "Mom, I love you and I am praying for you."

"I know you are. I love you too." I was so glad that I had the chance to tell her that I loved her. I wanted Jon and all our girls to know how much I loved them before I went through with this. We all said prayers together. We prayed for God to protect me and for the doctors to fix me.

The anesthesiologist came into the room and started to talk to me about my surgery. He then touched my face! Emily gasped. I immediately moaned and tears welled up in my eyes. He apologized. He decided that I would need to be knocked out even before going into the operating room.

One by one, my girls said their goodbyes to me and kissed me on the hand or on my right cheek. Tears were streaming down their faces. Jon was the last one, and I looked at him. His lips were quivering. Tears were spilling down his face. "I love you and you better wake up," he said. "I love you too." I hugged him and cried.

I was injected with the meds to make me go to sleep. The only thing that I remember is being wheeled into a cold room with many people around me. The next thing I remember, I woke up in a small recovery room. I was agitated and not myself. Jon, and all the girls, including Rachel, were there. I had no clue that it was already dark outside. It had been about ten hours.

Jon was so worried that my brain would be damaged that he decided to test me. Emily just changed her telephone number and so he asked me what it was. I rattled it off without hesitation. They were amazed and relieved.

Before I could go to my room, I had to have the catheter removed and use the bathroom myself. My daughter, Melissa, being a nurse, helped me with this since I had to use a bed pan and had never done that before.

While being wheeled to my hospital room, I told the nurse that I needed to be sick. I threw up twice. I was so out of it. I finally opened my eyes enough to notice that everything was double around me. I had to close my eyes because it was just so hard to handle. The doctor told me this would happen. Relax, you will be okay. It will go away, I told myself. I tried to look up, down, and just straight. Everything was double.

The surgery had lasted seven hours and there were two compressions, one being the whole length of my trigeminal nerve with an arterial vein "saran wrapped," as the doctor called it, to my nerve so he had to manipulate the nerve more than he had wanted to. There was also a blood vessel leaning on my left eye nerve, which he moved away as well. Mind you, he was working on nerves and vessels finer than a hair.

I was in the hospital for three days. Jon stayed with me. I was pretty drugged up that whole time, so I don't remember much. I do remember that our parish priest brought me Jesus twice while I was in the hospital. I was so happy to receive Jesus. Jesus brought me such consolation throughout this whole ordeal.

I had to use a walker because I was unsteady due to the double vision and from being weak from the surgery. Jon helped me go to the bathroom. I ended up staying in the hospital an extra day because I was so unsteady. How was I supposed to grab the correct handle on the door, or make sure I was stepping on the right step when I wasn't sure which of the two I was seeing was the real thing? At this time, I still didn't even know if the surgery had worked because of all of the other complications. I did have some break-through shocks and my head and my face were feeling like hot water then cold water was being thrown on it and then like bugs walking up my head. All this was from the manipulation of the nerve.

Finally, I was released on September 19. Jon wheeled me out in a wheelchair to the car. I was outside and the breeze did not bother me! The surgery had worked! I was still getting shocks though, so I was not entirely convinced, and I had a sensitivity to the bright light. Something else was going on too.

At home, I was not functioning very well. I kept on throwing up and the doctor didn't know why. I ended up going to the emergency room three times. I had a urinary tract infection from the catheter. I was constipated. My stomach seemed like it was not digesting my food. I was told that sometimes with long surgeries the organs get sluggish. I guess that is what happened to me.

I remember one instance clearly. A Eucharistic Minister from our church was bringing me Jesus on Sunday since I was not able to go to Mass. I tried to eat some breakfast but had to run to the bathroom and throw up. I started to cry. I knew what time I was supposed to receive Jesus and here I was throwing up. With tears coming down my face, I prayed, "Jesus, please let me be able to receive You when the person gets here, and please don't let me get sick after. I need You."

Jesus answered me because I was able to receive Him and didn't get sick again that day.

I slowly started to recover from this nightmare. There were days when I wished I hadn't woken up from the surgery. I am glad that I knew to offer all this up to God, so I did, but it wasn't joyfully.

After a few weeks, Emily, my youngest, said, "Mom, let's go sit on the porch." The thought of going outside again just to sit and enjoy the outdoors was so foreign to me. I was a little scared to open the door and take a step outside. I felt like I was taking another leap of faith. As I walked outside and sat down with my cup of coffee, Emily's eyes were glistening with tears—tears of relief that her mom was whole again. This moment in time would soon disappear like a long-lost friend. The sun seemed too bright, and I was having pain behind my eyes. I had to go back inside.

October 2, 2014 was my recheck with Dr. Mericle. My daughter, Melissa, came with me. Dr. Mericle told me that I had the worst case of Trigeminal that he has ever seen in all of the operations he has done. He said that my double vision and numbness should go away . . . but time proved that would not be the case. God, in His mercy, let my frontal vision return or else I would not have been able to do anything, but the rest of my vision is still double.

I kept thinking that I was running along the shores of Venice Beach last year at this time. How life can change in an instant!

If my surgery had been successful, why was I having so much pain and light sensitivity? Prior to surgery, I was told that something else was going on with the right side of my head. I went to a pain management specialist who diagnosed me with Occipital Neuralgia.

## OCCIPITAL NEURALGIA

Occipital Neuralgia (ON) is a condition in which the nerves that run from the top of the spinal cord to the scalp, called the occipital nerves, are inflamed or injured. You might feel pain in the back of your head or at the base of your skull.

People often think that they have migraines or other headaches because the symptoms are similar. The symptoms are: intense pain that feels like a sharp, jabbing, electric shock in the back of the head and neck. Aching, burning, or throbbing pain that starts at the bottom of the head and goes to the scalp. You can also have pain on one or both sides of your head, pain behind your eyes, a very tender scalp, and sensitivity to light.

On November 3, 2014, I had my first Radio Frequency Ablation (RFA), which is a procedure used to reduce pain. An electrical current produced by a radio wave is used to heat up a small area of nerve tissue, which decreases pain signals from that specific area.

The RFA was done on the right side of my head and it seemed to help the eye pressure. My head was not as cooperative. I sat in a dark room all the time because I had such light sensitivity. Ice packs on my head were the only relief besides over-the-counter pain medication.

Here it was, the holiday season. It would be Thanksgiving in a couple of weeks. I love to cook. My favorite memories are making dinner for my family. It's not what I cooked, it's the time that I spent with my children, especially since they were all grown and moved out except for Emily.

What I didn't know was that I would be facing a family tragedy in a few short weeks that would temporarily make me forget all my health troubles.

# CHAPTER 5: THE FIRST MAN THAT CALLED ME BEAUTIFUL
## 2014

*"We do not want you to be unaware, brothers, about those who have fallen asleep, so that you may not grieve like the rest, who have no hope. For if we believe that Jesus died and rose, so too will God, through Jesus, bring with him those who have fallen asleep."*
*—1 Thessalonians 4:13–14*

My father had cancer for many years. He was blessed to have a slow-growing renal cancer where he had to have a kidney removed when I was pregnant with my second daughter, Laura.

After fifteen years, his doctor retired and the new doctor decided to do more tests just to have an updated view on what was going on. My mother called me, sounding distraught. The first thing I thought of was my dad. "Cheryle, your dad has cancer again. He has a small tumor on his other kidney. Do not worry, he is scheduled to have surgery in a month to freeze the tumor."

I looked at Jon with wide eyes. He asked me what was the matter. I told him about Dad. Jon said that we needed to be there for the surgery. This surgery was before any of us had cell phones back in 2004.

We drove up to New York. When we got to the house, we knocked on the door. My mother answered the door with tears in her eyes. "What's wrong, Mom," I said. She told us that the PET scan showed a tumor the size of a softball on my dad's spleen and pancreas.

They delayed the surgery for another few weeks. I walked up the stairs, as my parents had a raised ranch at the time, and my eyes met my dad's; we both started to cry. I ran and hugged him. We stayed the time we planned and visited all of our family since we were there. Jon and I decided that I would fly up alone when Dad had his big surgery.

✠

Weeks later, I arrived the day before the surgery. We drove in silence to the hospital, Mom, Dad, and me. My sister and brother met us there. We said our goodbyes to Dad as he was prepped for surgery and went to the waiting room. We were pacing the floor. I pulled out my rosary and began to pray it.

Praying the rosary was new to me. I had learned how to pray the rosary from Mary and my church friends. All the time that I went to Catholic school, we never prayed the rosary. I think both of my grandmothers did, but I was never taught how to pray it.

While I was praying, I reflected on my childhood. My dad held a very active role in my upbringing. He was the one who dried my tears. One word from him could change my whole mood.

The surgery was long but successful. They managed to get all of the tumor, but the doctor had to remove half of his pancreas and all of his spleen. Dad became a diabetic.

After a few more years, the cancer returned, but this time it spread to his stomach. Dad knew he was living on borrowed time, but he did live ten more years. So many of his grandchildren and great-grand-children were born in those ten years. I thank God for the extra time Dad was able to be here.

My dad was my hero. He had a milder case of Trigeminal Neuralgia on top of having cancer. Believe it or not, we were both diagnosed the same week in two different states. Trigeminal Neuralgia is not hereditary but you can have the same physical anomalies as a family member, which can cause the defect to occur.

My dad understood me. He always understood me even before all this. He was the dad that told me I was beautiful. Any daughter loves to hear this from their dad.

About two weeks before my surgery, the phone rang. It was Dad. I answered the phone with apprehension. I said, "Hi, Dad, how are you doing?" He said, "Cheryle, I am going to stop taking the chemo drugs." I held my breath and said a silent prayer. "Dad," I answered, "quality of life is more important than quantity of life." I couldn't believe I had just said that to my dad. I didn't want to let him go, but I also didn't want to be selfish. He had already suffered so much.

He told me that he was right with God and at peace. "I am ready whenever He is. I am done fighting. I have had a great life." His only heartache was that he hated to see me in so much pain. He would often tell me that he would rather suffer for me. Anyone who has children understands this.

Since I live in Tennessee and my parents live in New York, I was not able to see them prior to my surgery, but my dad talked to me over the phone. He was so happy that my surgery had been successful. He was still concerned about my occipital neuralgia. He knew now I was able to go out of the house, but because of the eye sensitivity, which caused major pain, I was still a prisoner inside. Only this time, I had to close all my curtains and sit in darkness.

My parents lived half the year in a retirement community in Florida with many of their friends from New York. People in Florida affectionately call those who come from cold-weather states for the winter, Snow Birds. They had been doing this for many years. When they used to drive there, they would sometimes stop to see us. Due to Dad's health, flying became a better alternative.

I talked to my mom on the phone prior to their trip. She told me that Dad was insistent on leaving early this year. They were in Florida by the end of October.

It was early in the morning on November 22, 2014 when the phone rang. I was still in bed. I heard the trembling voice of my mom on the other end. "Cheryle, your dad is in the hospital. He threw up blood at home. The ambulance took him to the hospital and he had to have emergency surgery on his stomach."

I was disoriented and trying to digest what she was saying. I told her that we would come down there. My mom didn't want to face the fact that my dad could possibly be dying. She didn't want us to travel since I'd had surgery two months prior.

I hurriedly called my sister and brother to tell them the news. Mom had already called them. They weren't convinced that there was nothing to worry about. It was decided since I lived closer to Florida, that Jon and I would leave immediately. I was thankful to God that my surgery had been successful because I was able to drive to Florida without too much pain.

We made it to the hospital and my dad was in bad shape. He was hooked up to a ventilator. The nurse was trying to bring him around and she shouted to Dad, "Your daughter, Cheryle, is here." I was holding his hand and he couldn't even grip it. My dad was always a big, strong man. I knew this was not good. Finally, he struggled to open his eyes and looked right at me. I could tell by his expression that he had been waiting for me.

The nurse asked us to take my mom home since she had been there for so long. The nurse took down Mom's cell phone number and we went to the house. The nurse kept insisting that Dad was stabilized and we could take Mom home to rest and get cleaned up. We thought that we would be right back in the morning.

Apparently, the nurse called several times in the early morning hours but my mom was so exhausted that she didn't hear the phone calls. When we finally got the messages, we sped to the hospital. My mom was in disbelief. The messages said that my dad had coded.

It seemed like it took forever to get there. My mother was so distraught that she was not conveying the directions clearly for poor Jon who was driving.

We got there ten minutes too late. There was my dad, laying there with the tube still in his mouth . . . gone. What can you say or do when you see your parent, the strong man who you looked up to, lying motionless? My stomach was in knots. It was hard to breath. Such a surreal moment. The tears started to flow. I prayed for him under my breath and tried to console my mother.

I tried to hold my dad's hand, but it was already cold and so was his arm. I was trying to find somewhere on him that made me feel like he was still with me. I felt his shoulder, and it was still warm. I just caressed his shoulder for about ten minutes and told him that I loved him and I would miss him. I was so glad that his suffering was over.

I hadn't been around when my grandparents passed. We came up for the funeral, but we were not at their deathbed. Dad told me that it had been hard to be there at the time of death for them. Dad had a sensitive, loving heart, despite his large and scary demeanor. Jon had been afraid of him the first time that he met him. I told him that my dad is a big teddy bear. My dad always said that he didn't want anyone there when he died. I guess God granted him this request.

We came back home from Florida; it was Thanksgiving. Nobody felt like eating. It was a very somber time. I just kept thinking about my dad. We tried to talk about all the funny stories we could remember about him to change the mood.

After Dad's death, I felt so all alone. He was the only one who really understood what I was going through. Even though he had a milder case of TN, having cancer on top of it was even more of a struggle. It's hard to explain, but when you suffer, suddenly many things don't matter anymore. We get so caught up in the temporal challenges of life that we forget that we are not made for this world. We are made for heaven.

I became more aware of the Holy Souls in Purgatory. Can you imagine being so close to Heaven but not being able to attain it? I always had Masses said for my relatives, but now I had a profound sense of how the holy souls rely on our prayers. My devotion continued to grow for all of my loved ones. I also prayed for those who have nobody to pray for them.

# CHAPTER 6: DEALING WITH AN UNWELCOMED GUEST
## 2014–2016

*"Consider it all joy, my brothers, when you encounter various trials, for you know that the testing of your faith produces perseverance."*
—James 1:2–3

I think that the stress and trauma from my dad's passing caused my ON pain to get even worse. I actually had to schedule a nerve block on Christmas Eve, which didn't even work. I spent the whole day with ice packs on my head for Christmas.

I had been sleeping in a recliner since before my brain surgery in 2014 until June of 2015 when we bought an adjustable bed. That adjustable bed was a blessing from God. It was our children's idea and they chipped in to buy it. What a gift!

I had to sleep with my head raised because the pressure to lay my head down flat added to the pain. I used to tell Jon that I felt like there was a boulder on my head and someone was pushing on it.

My ON would flare up, but it wasn't constant pain yet so I was able to steal a few days here and there of pain relief. Then the pain came back with a vengeance. I was beginning to feel like I was going down this dark hallway toward a light that kept moving farther and farther away.

Since the ON pain was worsening, my pain management doctor suggested that I have another Radio Frequency Ablation. But instead of easing the pain, it intensified it. My head felt like hot coals were being thrown on it and the sparks were flying everywhere. Imagine my devastation at being told the procedure would definitely help me only to have it fail. I would start to have hope only to have it snatched away from me. "Sorry, there is nothing else I can do for you," my doctor

✙

eventually said. I cried all the way home. Was this going to be my life forever, God? Am I supposed to keep trying to get better or should I just give up?

Again, my support group told me of a procedure that would excise my nerves and stop the pain. God, in His mercy, guided me to look for a surgeon who could do this procedure. I would have total numbness on the right side of my head, but at that point, I had numbness on the left side of my face and double vision, why would I care to add numbness on my head?

I found a doctor in Virginia who could perform the surgery. Unfortunately, my insurance did not cover it due to out-of-state restrictions. I was devastated. What was I supposed to do now? I prayed: Lord, why did You have me learn about this surgery only to not provide a surgeon to do it?

I started to cry thinking about continuing to live in this pain. Staying in a dark room trying not to move or talk, I read a lot and prayed many rosaries. I kept praying that I could find another doctor to do this type of surgery for me.

I scoured the Internet. Again, God allowed me to find a doctor in Knoxville, Tennessee who took my insurance and would agree to meet with me on Skype first. I was elated. I thanked God and Mary. I had hope that maybe I would be pain-free. I had already forgotten what that felt like.

When I arrived at the doctor's office the day before the surgery, he examined me. "Mrs. Miller," he said, "the brain surgery that you had caused scar tissue to wrap around your occipital nerve on the left side too. I think this is why you have so much pain in your eyes along with your sensitivity to light." The surgery would take even longer, because both sides of my occipital nerves needed to be cut.

On November 6, I had the surgery. When I woke up, I couldn't feel my head. "Jon, I need you to move my pillow because I don't think it is behind my head," I said nonchalantly. "Your head is in the middle of the pillow." Jon showed me where my head was, and I couldn't feel it. The only way that I knew my pillow was under my head was by feeling it with my shoulders. It took me a long time to get used to this numbness. On the left-hand side, my head felt like a rock. The right side wasn't as bad. The best part was that after it healed, I had no pain!

The last Skype check-up I had with my doctor was in February 2016. He was so happy to see me without pain. I told him that I felt 100 percent better. He then said something to me that I thought I would never hear. "I want you to start reducing your medication now." I was so happy!

I started to slowly reduce my Trileptal. The first few months seemed to go fine. But at the end of April, out of nowhere, I got a small shock on my face. I didn't think anything of it. Then, I got another and another. The shocks were growing stronger.

There had been a 50/50 chance that my Trigeminal surgery would fail. After the doctor told me how bad my compression was, I had an uneasy feeling that maybe things would go awry. I was in a panic and decided to go back on my medication. This seemed to help a little bit, but the shocks continued.

I was in disbelief. Surely this was just a reaction to the medication. Still in denial, I was shopping at Aldi on a beautiful summer day when a sudden storm blew in with the roar of thunder and flashes of lightning. I had just checked out and was about to walk outside, oblivious of the pouring rain. I stood under the canopy and waited for the rain to subside enough for me to make a dash for the car. The breeze was warm but strong.

Finally, there was a break in the intensity of the rain so I ran to my car, dragging along my full grocery cart. The droplets of rain fell all around me and then one hit the left side of my face. My face started to burn! I felt like I was in a minefield waiting for the next bomb to detonate. I tried to pack all the groceries in the car and dodge the rain bullets. The pain was so intense that I was shaking.

I started to drive home but the pain would not let up. I felt like someone just took the first layer of skin off the left side of my face. I had to pull over at a gas station close to my home. I called my daughter Laura and her husband Matt, who lived close-by, to come and drive the car home. I also needed gas and couldn't get out in that rain minefield again. Laura said that when she got to me, I was shaking and my face was beet red like it had been burned. My Trigeminal was back with even more intensity. I had no clue that I could feel even more pain that I had felt prior to my surgery. Lord, I asked, how can I endure this pain? I need You.

Those few months of no pain felt like a prized possession that was thrown into the depths of the ocean never to be seen again. Think about how it feels to get a shock from static and multiply it by a thousand, maybe a million. My whole head would jump. I tried to control it but couldn't. People would look at me weird. Could you just imagine the intensity of pain that is to make your head jump like that? I would barely recover when another one would happen.

By September, I continued to get more pain and constant shocks. I started to cover my face with a cover that you would normally wear to keep dust off while dirt biking. I was so humiliated when people stared at me. This was the only way that I could leave my house or be around anyone. Jon had to walk slowly around me because just the air from him walking by me would cause so many shocks. I could hardly eat. I lost twenty-five pounds in three months because it hurt to even open my mouth.

I remember one night near Thanksgiving of 2016, having shock after shock for a couple of hours. The pain was so bad that I took more medication and even tried to numb it with some alcohol, but nothing touched it. I was praying my rosary and praying for the Lord to calm it down.

The next day, I called my neurologist. Sobbing, I said, "Please, I can't take this pain anymore, I need something to help me!" He prescribed two other medications. I've never been one to do well on medication. I am allergic to about four.

These two medications made me feel like a walking zombie. I was slurring my speech; I couldn't think straight. Despite all of these side effects, neither one lessened the pain. Emily was so worried about me. When she came over that night and saw the condition I was in, she was horrified.

The next day, I couldn't get out of bed. I tried many times to forcefully push myself up. I was just so weak that I could barely go to the bathroom. The pain was unbearable.

My friend Mary lived a block away from me. She would come over and check on me. She would bring me homemade soup to eat for lunch. I was so thankful for her love and care of me. She is a true friend that I love as a sister.

The days dragged on. One day in bed, then two, three, until I was in bed for two weeks straight. Jon was working long hours. He was forced to work mandatory overtime despite having a sick wife at home. I was home alone. I cried and cried for help but the days marched on like a soldier going into battle. I didn't want to startle my girls, so I never told them.

In my grief and solitude, I started to pray the rosary and just cry to Mother Mary about all of my problems and that's when something miraculous happened

One day I asked my friend Mary to pray for me. I woke up in the middle of the night to a very strong scent of roses in my room. Jon was sleeping, so I didn't want to wake him. I looked everywhere for what could have been the source of that scent but nothing explained it. People would often smell the scent of roses if Mother Mary was near. She was letting me know that she was near. She was holding my hand, gentle, loving mother that she is.

In that two-week span, every day I would pray rosary upon rosary, and I kept hearing, "You need to go to the dentist." Nobody listened to me, including my dentist. "It's just your Trigeminal pain," he said. I don't blame him since that is how I was diagnosed in the first place, because of the pain in my teeth. I just continued to pray the rosary. I heard it again, but with even more firmness, "You need to go to the dentist."

Finally, Emily suggested that I go to a natural dentist. The one I wanted to go to was booked out several months. I decided to just skip the dentist and go straight to an oral surgeon because I heard, in prayer, that my teeth needed to be pulled. Laura asked her dentist for suggested oral surgeons. I randomly picked one, but nothing is really random.

My appointment was the next day. I just barely rolled out of bed, got dressed, and drove there. My hair was everywhere as it had been many days since I'd showered. I couldn't stand up long enough on my own. Jon was working late, and I was usually sleeping by the time he got home. I didn't want to ask one of my girls to help me. I don't think any of them know how bad I really was to this day.

My Mama Mary sent me to an oral surgeon who has a mild case of Trigeminal Neuralgia. She understood. She was so sweet to me. When she took my x-rays, I had two bad root canals that were infected. One showed up totally black on the x-ray! This was what was causing the extra pain! If Mama Mary had not have been insistent that I go to the oral surgeon, I could have died from those infections. We met a man when we first moved here that told us about his daughter who'd died because she never took care of a bad tooth. That always stuck with me.

When my teeth were removed, I felt better. I could get out of bed. I still had my Trigeminal pain but the extra pain from having two bad teeth was gone. I couldn't wait to go back to church! I told my friends that Mother Mary was the one who guided me to the oral surgeon. The surgeon didn't even charge me to remove my teeth because she felt so bad for me. My Mother Mary took care of me.

# CHAPTER 7: WHERE IS GOD IN ALL OF THIS?
## 2016

*"Come to me, all you who labor and are burdened, and I will give you rest. Take my yoke upon you and learn from me, for I am meek and humble of heart; and you will find rest for yourselves. For my yoke is easy, and my burden light." —Matthew 11:28-30*

After my teeth were taken care of, I started going back to daily Mass. Every First Friday, our priest would have Adoration of the Blessed Sacrament until noon.

Adoration of the Blessed Sacrament is sitting with Jesus. Adoring Him and praising Him in His Eucharistic form, meaning the consecrated host. The host is put into a holder called a Monstrance. Catholics adore and venerate our Eucharistic Lord. The King of kings and Lord of lords wanted to stay with us. He wanted to constantly feed us the bread of life. When we look at Our Lord in the form of the Eucharist, we see His humility.

Before I was sick, I was always on the go, and sitting still for even ten minutes seemed unbearable. I didn't know how to pray or what to do when in Adoration. I never stopped long enough to be silent. Jesus, in His mercy, even though I didn't realize it at the time, took me off that hamster wheel of life and gave me the gift of Himself.

I was in so much pain that I kept begging Jesus to take it away. I was scared, mad, and felt abandoned. It was made more frustrating because not everyone in my family believed me. I wanted to cry out, "Why would I make up this kind of pain?"

We had this beautiful statue on the altar of the Sacred Heart of Jesus that I would stare at during daily Mass or in First Friday Adoration. At that time, I didn't know anything about the First Friday devotion or about the promises of the Sacred Heart of Jesus.

The First Friday devotion to the Sacred Heart of Jesus came from private revelation of Jesus to St. Mary Margaret Alacoque. Jesus wished the devotion to His Sacred Heart be more known. Through her encounters with Christ, she helped establish a feast day and the Nine First Fridays Devotion. Every first Friday of the month for nine months, the faithful go to Mass and receive the Eucharist and say a prayer for reparation for offenses made against the Sacred Heart. Jesus promises the following to those that keep this devotion:

I will give them all the graces necessary for their state of life.
I will give peace in their families.
I will console them in all their troubles.
I will be their refuge in life and especially in death.
I will abundantly bless all their undertakings.
Sinners shall find in my Heart the source and infinite ocean of mercy.
Tepid souls shall become fervent.
Fervent souls shall rise speedily to great perfection.
I will bless those places wherein the image of my Sacred Heart shall be exposed and venerated.
I will give to priests the power to touch the most hardened hearts.
Persons who propagate this devotion shall have their names eternally written in my Heart.
In the excess of the mercy of my heart, I promise you that my all-powerful love will grant to all those who will receiv Communion on the First Fridays, for nine consecutive months, the grace of final repentance: they will not die in my displeasure, nor without receiving the sacraments; and my Heart will be their secure refuge in that last hour.

Once I learned of these promises, I tried to complete this devotion. I remember the many times I would pray so hard to go to First Friday Adoration. Many times, I would be so sick that I couldn't make it. Sometimes I would push myself out of bed, looking terrible, but still making it to see Jesus even if for a few minutes.

I began to meditate on Jesus' Passion and my friend, Mary, gave me the book by Father Michael Gaitley, *Consoling the Heart of Jesus*. I devoured this book because I am a simple soul and he writes for simple souls. This book is a weekend retreat based on the Spiritual Exercises of St. Ignatius of Loyola. Father Gaitley asks in the book if we would like to console Jesus for the suffering he went through for us. I wanted to make Jesus feel better. I offered up all of my sufferings to Him.

As I've explained, I didn't know my faith well, but I did learn to love Jesus. I looked at Jesus and I related to His Passion. I felt so abandoned and useless. In the midst of this, I fell in love with Jesus. He died on the cross for me. I didn't have to do anything or be anyone for Him to love me; He just did. *Why do you love me?* I always asked Him. *Why did you take up your cross willingly? How can we, as humans, really understand the depth of God's love for us?* We don't know how to love. Our love is clouded with selfishness, conditions, and expectations. It took me a while to actually accept His love, and I remember the day I did clearly.

It was December 4. This is the day when I had a life-changing grace given to me. I had to go to Mass by myself that day since Jon had to work. He went to Mass on Saturday night. I was having a lot of pain that day. I remember being in deep prayer with God just crying and asking for His mercy.

While I was walking up to receive the Eucharist, I heard in my heart, "Come to me." When I received Jesus, He filled me with such love that I thought my heart was going to burst. The pain that I had was lessened too. I couldn't stop crying because I had never felt anything like it. Suddenly, I knew that my God loved me. He has so much love for us. We just need to let Him in. All of my life, I felt like I had to earn love. If I didn't do everything perfect, I wasn't loved. There were always conditions. The Devil had me believing that nobody would love me just for being me.

I remember texting my friend Mary and telling her. The first time I actually understood that God loved me was when I was sick in bed for two weeks. I believed it in my head but had not yet accepted it in my heart. After this day, I knew that God loved me! Little, broken, despairing, me! No longer did I have to play the games, or try to fit in. God loved me! I could never do anything to earn His love because He already loved me. What a grace! My life was never the same after that.

I began to look at things in a new light. I read so many saints books that talked about the value of redemptive suffering. Jesus, in His mercy, allows us to offer our sufferings up to Him for the salvation of souls. Why He allows this, I don't know. He is God and could do it without us, but when we offer up our suffering, our lives have value.

I thought of myself as worthless because I couldn't do anything. I valued myself on the amount I could accomplish. The world does the same thing. If you are a wanted baby, it's okay that you survive. If you are not wanted, it's okay to kill it. *"It isn't a baby yet anyway,"* says the lying serpent. *"Oh, you are too old to do anything, why bother still living? Here, I will help you kill yourself. Oh, you are suffering so much, do you really want to continue with all that pain?"* says the serpent.

We live in the "valley of tears." We are supposed to suffer here so that our reward is great in Heaven. As crazy as it sounds, I started to enjoy my pain, in a sense. I offered it up for many people, including Jon and my children. I also offered it up for others I didn't know. My friend, Mary, called my suffering a "superpower." I felt like Super Woman. I couldn't hardly do a thing physically, but spiritually, I was rocking it!

I started to push my pain aside and go on with life as best as I could. I learned to endure it with as much eloquence as I could muster. God was preparing me for my next trial. A trial that would really put me to the test.

# Chapter 8: Jon's Heart Attack
## 2016

*"Do not let love and fidelity forsake you; bind them around your neck; write them on the tablet of your heart. Then will you win favor and esteem before God and human beings."*
*—Proverbs 3:3–4*

The world decided to stop on its axis on March 9, 2016. Reading back in my journal, I could sense the surrealness of that day.

Jon called me during his lunch time. He hadn't felt well the night before because he had this gas pain in his chest that wouldn't go away. Finally, it subsided and he was able to sleep. The next morning, he got up for work and told me that he felt better. I didn't give it another thought until he called me at lunch time. After he ate, the pain came back and it was accompanied by a pain in his jaw. I had no clue that it was his heart. He had high blood pressure and was on all these medicines, including a statin. His cholesterol levels were great, so we thought we had no reason to worry. Boy, were we wrong!

Jon is a diehard worker. I am very thankful for his work ethic, but when he told me that he was going to wait until the end of the day and stop by the doctor's office to see what he had to say, I was not sure that was such a smart idea. He minimizes his sicknesses, so I knew if he wanted to go to the doctor, it must be serious.

Three hours later, when work ended, he called me to say that he was going to the doctor's office. When he arrived, the doctor told him to go the emergency room because he is probably having a heart attack. In fact, the doctor said to the nurse on the phone when she called him from the front desk, "Tell the dummy to go to the emergency room." Mind you, Jon wasn't offended because he had a great relationship with our family physician. Thankfully, the hospital was just a short walk down a corridor from the doctor's office.

In the meantime, I contacted all of our girls, despite Jon's objections. I knew that they would want to be there. I contacted our priest through a friend of mine as well.

When I arrived at the hospital, they already had Jon hooked up to several monitors. One by one, our children showed up with panicked looks on their faces. Jon was not happy that I had "bothered" them.

The doctors on staff were friendly. They took blood and did some other tests on him. They even gave him a Nitroglycerine pill under his tongue. Nothing helped. Jon was in denial that he was having a full-blown heart attack. The doctor had to argue with him. "Mr. Miller, you are having a heart attack."

I looked around the room with almost all of our children and grandchildren present, Melissa was on her way. Some were crying, others were sitting quietly. I knew we had to pray. I surprised myself by holding it all together.

While they were getting the operating room ready, we prayed the Divine Mercy Chaplet together.

We started . . . *You expired Jesus but the source of life gushed forth for souls and the ocean of mercy opened up for the whole world . . . for the sake of His sorrowful Passion, have mercy on us and on the whole world.*

You could hear our prayer spilling out into the hall. We were praying for God's mercy on Jon. The nurses and doctors waited for us to finish. We said our goodbyes as everyone hurried up to give Dad/ Grandpa some sort of gesture, whether a quick kiss or touch. I waited until everyone left. I held Jon's hand as they started to move him out of the room and down the corridor. The male nurse was very nice. He stopped before he rolled him through the surgery doors and let me kiss him one more time. My heart was breaking. "Please, Lord, take care of Jon."

I joined my family in the waiting room. It was spacious with many chairs, but after we arrived, the size diminished. I took this opportunity to go into the women's bathroom, fall to the floor, and cry. I wanted to be strong for my children, but I just couldn't hold it back any longer. A flood of tears began to fall down my face. I was praying for God to save Jon.

Rachel came to get me because Melissa and the grandchildren had arrived. Melissa had a worried look on her face. Being a nurse, she knew that this was very serious.

Then our priest arrived. He was very sweet and prayed with me. My friend Mary and other people from our church showed up as well. I was glad to pass the time with my friends as every minute seemed endless. I had already endured brain surgery and nerve excision surgery and the loss of my dad. Jon is my other half. We do everything together. The thought of losing him, I just couldn't handle.

Suddenly, all of the years Jon and I shared came to mind like I was watching a movie. Our wedding, our first child, our first grandchild, and on and on. I also thought about how I just expected him to always be there. How much I regretted. I vowed to be a better wife.

When the doctor finally came into the room, he told me that Jon had had a 100 percent blockage in one of the arteries. The stent was able to clear the artery totally. He was amazed. I didn't really understand what he was saying, I just wanted to see my husband.

It was late at night by the time the surgery was over. I walked in to the room to find my happy husband, a little tipsy from the anesthesia. He looked at me and we were both so happy to just gaze in each other's eyes for a moment. He was still hooked up to machines. He was put in the intensive care unit to monitor overnight. I was hoping to sleep in the room with him, but I was not able to.

When I arrived in the morning, Jon was smiling. Deacon Simeon was there to visit him from church. He brought Jesus in the form of the Eucharist. Jon was like a new person.

☩

The following week, we had a follow-up appointment with the heart specialist. I made sure to go to because you know men, they never tell you the details. Anyway, the doctor was shaking his head in amazement still. He told us that he had never seen an outcome as good as Jon's. Usually there is some residual blockage or more that had to be done.

We knew why. God had intervened. We just don't understand the depth of His love for us.

His mercy is endless.

This is the ending prayer of the
Divine Mercy Chaplet:

*"Eternal God in whom mercy is endless and the treasury of compassion inexhaustible, look kindly upon us and increase Your mercy in us that in difficult moments we might not despair nor become despondent, but with great confidence submit ourselves to Your holy will, which is love and mercy itself."*

God used this experience to open my heart even more. Ever since I became ill, the focus was always on me. I always leaned on Jon. He was the rock that I depended on, the one who knew what I was going through more than anyone else. The tables were now turned. I had to push aside my pains to be there for him. In a way, God used this experience to show me to look beyond myself. Despite my illness, He wanted me to look at others first. He wanted me to put myself last.
*"So the last will be first, and the first last"* (Matt 20:16, ESV).

# CHAPTER 9: TWENTY-FOUR HOUR ADORATION
## 2016-2017

*"[H]e humbled himself, becoming obedient to death, even death on a cross. Because of this, God greatly exalted him and bestowed on him the name that is above every name, that at the name of Jesus every knee should bend, of those in heaven and on earth and under the earth, and every tongue confess that Jesus Christ is Lord, to the glory of God the Father."*
*—Philippians 2:8–11*

When I was at daily Mass or Adoration, I kept hearing the words "Perpetual Adoration" over and over in my heart. The Lord desired to have Adoration more often. I asked my priest three times over the span of a couple of years.

What I didn't know was that my friend Mary was asking him the same thing. Finally, Father allowed us to work together on this project. We knew that starting off with Perpetual Adoration would not happen in a church our size, only five hundred registered families, so we decided on twenty-four-hour Adoration. We prayed about how to handle this and Mother Mary guided us through it. We randomly picked Thursday as the day of the week to hold Adoration.

We started twenty-four-hour Adoration on June 1, 2017. June happens to be the month of the Eucharist. We found out later that since Holy Thursday is when Jesus gave us the Eucharist, Thursday is considered a day of Adoration. We had no idea, but Mother Mary did.

Mary and I were blessed to have a great support group from the parish. We had at least two people signed up for every hour and a few substitutes. There were about fifty-five or so very dedicated adorers.

The first few weeks, Mary and I spent many hours in Adoration to make sure everything was going smoothly and nobody forgot their time slot. It is so important not to leave Jesus alone. Would you leave your vulnerable child alone? I know that Jesus is God, but He allows Himself to be vulnerable in the form of the Eucharist. We both expressed the importance of always having someone present with Him. Jesus never wanted to leave us alone. He asked the Father if "where I am, they also may be" (John 17:24). He wanted to stay with us.

Every time I walked into Adoration, I would look at Jesus and think, What divine humility. I was so humbled to see all those in the room adoring Jesus in different ways.

A young Hispanic man would bring Jesus a vase of flowers every Thursday. He fell on his face in front of the Lord and ever so reverently left the vase of flowers underneath the small altar we had in our church cry room that was also used as the Adoration chapel.

Many women would come, wearing veils and praying the rosary. Some were crying and kneeling. Others were prostrated on the floor in deep prayer.

I was just outside the door about to walk in to the Adoration room one time when I heard the faint sound of children praying. As I opened the door, I saw many families from the church homeschool group kneeling and saying a decade of the rosary. Every child had a rosary from the oldest to the infants. Some of them even drew pictures for Jesus and left them under the altar. Tears welled up in my eyes to see the small acts of love that these children did for Jesus.

It was in this time that Jesus transformed my heart. I yearned for Him. I was able to spend as much time with Him as I could handle. I was always in the worst pain in front of Him for some reason. At first, I just thought it was me. I finally asked Him and He said to my heart, That is when you are most united to me. I am nothing, a nobody! Yet, Jesus, in His mercy, stooped down to me. He continues to guide and nurture me like a father does his little girl.

My job is to remember that I am little and that He expects me to mess up. Like a young child that trips and falls will run to their mother crying, I run to God. I know that He is the only one who will dry my tears. He is the only one who gives me peace. Peace that the world does not know. Like a young child trying to walk, I would keep getting up to take a step and then fall. Jesus would be right there to pick me up and hold my hand as I tried to take another tiny step.

I had come to understand the heart of Jesus. He is all love. His mercy for us goes beyond understanding. Look at the way that He treated the soldiers who beat and crucified Him. He looked at them with tender love. Instead of accepting this love, they beat Him all the more. Who can really understand the mercy of God? His mercy is so wide and vast that we would not be able to even comprehend the depth of it with our human minds. Sister Faustina would often refer to Divine Mercy as a huge ocean.

Jesus said to St. Faustina Kowalska from Poland, who was a nun, mystic, and Apostle of Divine Mercy who lived from 1905 to 1938. This is Diary #738 from her book, *Divine Mercy in my Soul.* Jesus said: *Without special help from Me, you are not even capable of accepting My graces. You know who you are.*

I learned how to love Jesus, but I didn't apply this love to others well. I still had a lot of growing to do in the "love your neighbor as yourself" area.

# Chapter 10: New House, New Town

2017–2019

*"I have indeed built you an exalted house, a place for you to dwell in forever."*
*—1 Kings 8:13, ESV*

My youngest daughter Emily was the only daughter still living at home while I was sick. I was diagnosed in 2014, when she was twenty. Emily is a sensitive young girl with a heart full of love. She always wanted to help me clean and spend time with me. When I was diagnosed and as my illness progressed, she helped me. Even though she was working full time, she managed to check in on me when Jon was working.

One morning, I was sleeping on the recliner and Emily crept up to me. The way that she tells the story is that she was getting ready for work. She kept coming out of the bathroom into the living room, looking at me. Her heart started to race, "Mom, are you okay?" I startled awake, in awful pain. The only relief from pain was sleeping, but as soon as I woke up, it would rush in like a roaring lion ready to devour me. Emily was in tears. "Mom, I thought you weren't breathing."

After she left for work, I just cried knowing the trauma that I was putting my daughter through. I didn't involve my other girls too much because I didn't want them to worry about me like Emily did. What a gut- wrenching experience for a young girl to see her mom so sick. She would go to work and her coworkers would talk about who went out on a date, what movie they watched, and there was Emily, worrying about what might greet her when she got home.

Emily met Levi, a wonderful young man who actually worked with my oldest daughter, Melissa, at a nursing home as a nurse. He has a sweet, servant's heart. They got married on August 27, 2016.

Although Emily moved out, she called me all the time and came over often. She was still so worried about me. They lived in an apartment for a year. About that time, we lived in a huge, three-thousand-square-foot home. I was not capable of taking care of myself, let alone a huge house. We decided to sell the house for a smaller, more manageable one.

Emily called me one day and said, "Mom, we want to help Dad take care of you, so we can all live together." My first reaction was a resounding yes, but then I thought about it. We had owned six houses over the course of our thirty-seven years of marriage. Living together meant that Emily wouldn't be able to move unless we wanted to move too. She decided that she would take that risk if it meant she could help take care of me.

We prayed about whether to build or buy a new house. Emily and I would drive all over trying to find houses. Two of our bids fell through for other houses and properties that came available in the fast-paced real estate market we have in Tennessee. We were getting discouraged.

Levi's family lives in a town about an hour away from where Jon and I lived. At that time, driving more than a half hour caused excruciating pain. Since we kept getting nowhere trying to find a house, Emily and Levi made a decision. Emily called and said, "Mom, we are just going to rent a house from Levi's family next door to their house."

I just cried to the Holy Mother. I will never be able to see my grandchildren! I couldn't drive an hour away. I decided to pray the Sorrowful Mother Chaplet and offer up my heartache to Mother Mary, knowing that her heart was in so much pain standing at the foot of the cross. I united my small suffering to hers and accepted what would happen.

Prior to this decision, Emily and I had been driving around in different areas. I noticed a road with a biblical name in a small town next to mine. I said, "That's a good biblical name, we need to remember this road."

Hoping and praying, I continued to check the real estate ads and a house became available on the road with the biblical name. The listing picture showed a very big house. I never opened the listing to look at it fully. I saw this house listing for four days before I heard, "Open it." I am sure that was Mother Mary.

There was the house and huge garage and an RV garage that would be great for my husband's workshop. The huge garage could be converted into living space. I hurried and called Emily and told her to check out the listing. There were several pictures. It was too good to be true. Emily wanted to look at it right away.

Emily and I went to look at it ourselves since both of our husbands were working. We drove down the road, with the many beautiful houses, and we pulled up to the house. From the outside, we could see it was rustic with fieldstone rock work accenting the barnwood exterior. The porch had an old wooden porch swing. Emily just fell in love with it. When we went inside, the beauty continued. Rock work enhanced both the living room and dining room. The living room has a vaulted ceiling with gray barnwood going around the fireplace, also made out of fieldstone. The warmth and rustic feel just overpowered both of us.

We then went in to the "garage." It was a total of over 2,600 square feet with three garage doors. The previous owner used to paint vehicles. Emily and I looked at it and suddenly the whole design of my future house came into my mind. There was a lot of work that needed to be done to convert this garage into a house.

One of my stipulations was to live close to church and this house was twenty minutes away. I wasn't so sure because I was used to driving five minutes to church. I kept praying and praying and finally, five days later, we put a low offer in and they took it! We were shocked!

Since we had so many variables to this house purchase, it was complicated. Our closing was scheduled two days before Emily's birthday in April. At the closing, after the paperwork was signed, the financial advisor said to me, "Someone up there must be watching over you." I didn't understand what he was saying. He went on to explain that he was almost going to call me to cancel the closing because all the paperwork was not in order. Just before he called, everything showed up the last minute. I knew who was watching over us. The love of a mother knows no boundaries, especially when that mother is the Queen of Heaven.

When we closed on the house, we had to sell our house before we could move in. Emily and Levi moved in April and we didn't move in until the end of June 2017, after our house sold. Since the garage had to be remodeled, more like overhauled, we lived in the house with Emily and Levi. The small bedroom that we stayed in just barely fit the adjustable bed.

Jon had the job of turning the garage into a house. He had done it before. Jon is an amazing woodworker. He knows everything there is to know about wood. St. Joseph and Jesus gave him their trade and what he can do is amazing. I have a beautiful kitchen made by him as well.

Jon was overwhelmed to have to start over again. We were in our late fifties, and it just didn't appeal to him to have to remodel a garage into a house. Unfortunately, many of our plans changed as sickness took over. We had planned to travel a lot when all of our children moved out and here we were moving in with one of them.

Today, we both love being here. We get to see two of our daughters because our third daughter, Rachel, went through an unexpected divorce and moved in with us. I can't tell you the blessings that I have received from being around two of my daughters all the time. I truly wish that my older daughters would move close to us too.

We are a part of their lives. A part that I would have never been able to be due to my health limitations. Throughout this time, my pain got worse, and I had to spend many days in bed. I felt so alone despite being surrounded by my family. Nobody really understands a day in the life of someone with chronic pain unless you have experienced it yourself. I couldn't relate to anyone, not even Jon. Jon was busy working at his job and then working on our house. Emily had her first child in July of 2017. I managed to make Adoration as much as I was able. Then I took a turn for the worse.

My pain level was going up so the doctor raised my medication to the toxicity level. This caused many side effects. I started to wake up in the middle of the night with gas pain in my stomach. At first, my family physician thought I was having gallbladder issues. I went in for all the tests and nothing showed up. I was perplexed. Here I go again, down this road of a barrage of tests to find out that there is nothing wrong with me. If that was the truth, then why did I throw up while they were releasing me from the hospital? I didn't know what to do. I prayed for guidance. The medical community had given up on me. I felt like I was stuck in the middle of the ocean and the only ship around was the Titanic.

I was a throw-away object; I didn't fit the mold; I wasn't productive; I was worthless. The Devil told me numerous times how worthless I was. Remember, I've always thought I had to earn love, had to do or be something to be loved. I had fallen for the Devil's games too many times in the past. I was not going to let him win again.

I turned to God and in His mercy. He brought me down the path of an unexpected remedy.

# Chapter 11: Alternative Medicine
## 2018-2020

*"Along each bank of the river every kind of fruit tree will grow; their leaves will not wither, nor will their fruit fail. Every month they will bear fresh fruit because the waters of the river flow out from the sanctuary. Their fruit is used for food, and their leaves for healing."*
*—Ezekiel 47:12*

My stomach issues were not getting any better. I was praying about what to do, and Emily's mother-in-law, Jeanna, suggested that I go to a natural doctor to seek help. The doctor lived in Alabama but would talk to me over the phone. Finally, I had hope.

This doctor didn't diagnose me but, by examining a sample of my hair, made suggestions on how to fix the mineral deficiencies in my body.

The medication the neurologist had prescribed made me gain about fifty pounds. He warned me that this type of medicine would do this. I also had a tendency to eat sweets. I've since learned how bad sugar is for you. I didn't know that sugar actually feeds cancer cells and causes inflammation in your body. I had a lot to learn.

My doctor suggested a vigorous diet. I juiced and ate a 90 percent raw diet of fruits and vegetables. The only meat I could eat was fish and some grass-fed beef. He started me on many supplements and oils. He suggested I do coffee enemas. I had never heard of that and at first, thought, I am not doing that. I started everything but the enemas.

I was extremely sick and couldn't keep anything down, which he expected. He said that with all the toxins in my system due to the amount of medication that I took for my ON and being on anti-convulsant medication, I had to get rid of all of this in my system. I started to read more and more about natural medicine and embraced it.

I also read how long certain medications stay in our systems. It was an eye-opener to me. He also said that the coffee enemas would help to get rid of the toxins faster. So, I started to do the coffee enemas, which surprisingly, made me feel better.

My doctor always had a positive outlook, showing me success stories of people being cured of MS and other nerve type diseases. He told me that I would be totally healed of not only my stomach issues but my Trigeminal within nine months. Dare I believe him? Do I dare allow myself to get on that emotional roller coaster of hope again?

I kept what he said in the back of my mind, but didn't count on it. The months dragged out to more than two years. My stomach issues were gone and I'd lost weight, but I had also lost hope that my Trigeminal would be healed.

Today, my diet is not 90 percent raw fruits and vegetables, and I don't juice very often, but I still keep most of the principles of no meat, sugar, processed foods, fast foods, etc. I have lost over seventy-five pounds. This helped my body endure the Trigeminal pain easier, despite its insistent continuation.

## CHIROPRACTIC CARE

*"Do you not know that your body is a temple of the holy spirit within you, whom you have from God, and that you are not your own? For you have been purchased at a price. Therefore, glorify God in your body."*
—*1 Corinthians 6: 19-20*

I kept reading on my Facebook support group page that people were having success with chiropractors, so I decided to go to one that my daughter, Rachel, suggested. Rachel was seeing him and receiving good results. His name is Dr. Evan Pridmore. He does what is called the torque-release technique. Using a spring-loaded instrument that looks like a pen, when released it only touches the areas of the spine that need to be worked on. It is less invasive and more accurate than hand manipulation.

I read an article about how chiropractic care on your neck can alleviate Trigeminal pain, which matched up with what my support group was saying. Finally, I read something encouraging, but I didn't get my hopes up too high since I have been on that roller coaster before.

I learned so much about my spine, which includes the head and neck, where my problems were. I didn't know that subluxations are when the spine is misaligned and pushing on a nerve. Those nerves in our spine control the rest of our body. If they are not aligned properly, especially over a period of years, damage can occur in other parts of our body that those nerves control. I was fascinated. I always thought that chiropractors were just good for back aches. I never knew that just like going to the doctor for regular check-ups, you should also go to your chiropractor for regular adjustments. Adjustments are when the spinal bones are put back in place again because as we live and move, we misalign these bones.

I was always impressed with a sign in his office that showed a picture of a rubber band cutting off the circulation on a finger. Some of the options to fix it were to medicate it, cut it, stretch it . . . or you could just remove the rubber band. I have read testimonies in his office about people who were not able to walk who then try chiropractic care and put their walkers away. People who have had many back surgeries finally finding relief. One autistic child hated water and now he swims and wants to take baths. Women who have irregular cycles or fertility issues become regular and are able to conceive. Mine is one of the testimonies because he really helped me be able to move better and have more energy.

Due to pain, my neck and back were so rigid. When I slept, I was using my neck and back as a pillow for my head, not allowing the slightest pressure on my head due to pain. I had no clue that I was doing this. It was my body's reaction to pain. Because of this, my body hardly ever touched the mattress. I had to physically tell myself to relax and then push my shoulders, back, arms, and legs on the mattress.

I started to see some benefits from chiropractic care. I was able to lower my bed down some because the neck and back didn't have to hold up the head so much. I was able to rotate my neck without pain. My body, as a whole, felt stronger. I had so many layers of problems that needed to be addressed in addition to the main culprits. I also have arthritis in my neck, hands, and feet.

I would highly recommend chiropractic care for prevention. My grandchildren have gone ever since they were born. My daughter Emily's second birth was so easy due to the care that Dr. Evan gave her. He specializes in a technique that helps pregnant women stay aligned throughout pregnancy.

Even though I was making tremendous strides in the rigidity of my body due to the pain, the pain continued. I learned never to take life for granted. I learned to live like I was dying.

Every day I would get up and thank God for the day. If I was able to get out of bed, I would go to daily Mass and just sit with Jesus. I always pondered on His Passion. The awful pain that he must have felt in his head from the thorns. How could I keep crying and whining when my Lord went through that for me?

## OTHER REMEDIES

My pain management specialist decided to try an SPG block, which is supposed to immediately stop pain. He had good results with it from his other Trigeminal patients. When the day came to have this nerve block, Emily came with me. She was so excited because she read that this nerve block works well. She thought for sure that I would be walking out the door pain-free. I, on the other hand, was not so sure.

I had been down this road before . . .

Sphenopalatine ganglion is a group of nerve cells inside your nose that is linked to the Trigeminal nerve. The doctor uses lidocaine on a long catheter-type Q-tip and then puts the Q-tip up the nose so that it touches the SPG nerves. The first time he inserted the Q-tip, I felt no relief. He tried a second time and still nothing. My doctor was stumped. He thought for sure that this would work. Emily was disappointed. I somehow knew that this would happen. I tried to guard my heart, but I still cried all the way home inside, trying not to show any emotion to Emily.

My next appointment with the pain specialist was the following week. He did some research and suggested a nerve stimulator be implanted in my back to stop the electrical impulses to my head.

I had to have a psychological evaluation prior to the implant. After the evaluation, I received a phone call. "Mrs. Miller, I am afraid that we cannot have the stimulator implanted because your insurance won't cover the procedure." My heart sank. I asked the nurse if she knew of any other options. She said that she would call me right back after she spoke to the doctor.

I started to pace the floor and pray the rosary. It felt like hours before she called me back, though it was only about fifteen minutes. "Mrs. Miller, I asked the doctor and he said that he is out of options for you. He wants to see you in the office in six months. I called in your prescription for your medication." The only thing that I remembered saying was "thank you" before hanging up. I felt like someone had punched me in the stomach. Holding back tears, I just went to my room and got in bed in the middle of the day, praying and crying.

The next morning, I got up and prayed for strength. I had exhausted all measures. I tried every avenue offered to me, but this pain would not be removed from me by any man-made intervention. This pain would be my constant companion for the rest of my life. Jesus, in His divine mercy, carried me like a stray lamb with a broken leg.

# Chapter 12: Consecrations

*"Most blessed are you among women, and blessed is the fruit of your womb"* —Luke 1:42

## TO JESUS THROUGH MARY

God used Father Michael Gaitley's books throughout my spiritual journey to grow my faith. I am, by far, not done growing, but at a critical time, his books really opened my heart. I am a very simple person, not learned, especially in the faith. Father Gaitley has a way of writing that even I can understand. After reading Consoling the Heart of Jesus, I started reading 33 Days to Morning Glory.

A consecration means you dedicate yourself to a specific purpose or plan. In this case, all of our prayers, sacrifices, fasting to Jesus, go through the beautiful, motherly hands of Mary.

Mary gave birth to Jesus. She nurtured him and raised him just like any other child would be raised. She knows Him better than anyone. It makes sense that we would give her everything of ours—prayers, merits (meaning your good deeds)—so she can present them to Jesus and distribute at her discretion.

You may be thinking, *I want to pray for who I wish to pray for.* You can still do this. The difference is that Mother Mary will take these prayers and gifts, give them to who needs them most, and because you freely allowed her to do this, she will also take care of your family and whomever you wish to pray for. She is never outdone in generosity.

Father Gaitley said throughout the book that when you are consecrated to Jesus through Mary, your life will change.

I started to notice my life changing very subtly. Mother is very gentle. When I would pray the rosary, she would tell me nice things that I could do for others or she would give me peace. On days when my pain level was off the charts, she comforted me. I would ask her to hold my hand or cover me with her mantle. She is a beautiful mother. She taught me how to let go of my pain by looking through the eyes of others in pain. She always gave me chances to help others who were suffering. I understood their pain. Thinking of others and helping them in small ways comforted me.

I consecrated all of my children to Mother Mary. I see how she is working in my girls' lives. Praying the rosary changes lives. Mary wants to help us. She knows the pains and sorrows that we go through. Remember her sorrows at the foot of the cross? I don't know how she stood there for three hours. Saying nothing. Crying. Seeing the pain that her Son was in, not being able to console Him. She prayed for us at the foot of the cross. She wants all of us to come to Jesus to console His heart. She loves us like only a mother can love. She is just waiting for your "yes." She will fly to you and never leave your side.

## CONSECRATION TO MERCIFUL LOVE

*"The Lord is gracious and merciful, slow to anger and abounding in love."*
*—Psalm 145:8*

The next book that I read is called 33 Day Consecration to Merciful Love also by Father Michael Gaitley.

In this book, Father Gaitley talks about St. Therese of Lisieux. She is better known as the Little Flower. Both of my grandmothers had a devotion to her, but I didn't know who she was.

When I read this book, I thought, there is hope for me yet! St. Therese is famous for her "Little Way" to holiness. Her little way is not that little since she is a Doctor of the Church. It is a path to holiness that anyone can travel, even me.

I knew that I was lacking in knowledge. I learned a lot since I moved to Tennessee, but it would take me a lifetime to learn all that the church has to offer and here I was in my fifties. I had wasted so much time with useless things. I felt the urgency to learn and grow despite my illness. I want to become a saint, but how was that possible? I don't know anything, and I am sick, but I could love Jesus.

How did St. Therese tell us to love Jesus? She said that we must become like a little child. Jesus said in the Gospel of Matthew: *"Amen, I say to you, unless you turn and become like children, you will not enter the kingdom of heaven" (18:3).* Therese understood that for her love offerings to be valuable, she needed to stay small. Slowly, and after reading her books a few times, it really sunk in to me what she was trying to say.

Our God is an Almighty God, creator of *everything*! He is big and we are small. Yes, we are very small. So small that we can't do a thing on our own. We have to have child-like trust. What is child-like trust? I live with three of my nine grandchildren and see examples of child-like trust regularly. One day, my grandson, Joshua, was walking down the stairs. When Joshua saw me at the bottom of the stairs with my arms opened wide to catch him, without hesitation, he let go of the railing and fell into my arms. What trust! He knew that I was his grandma who loved him and would catch him. That's it! Child-like trust! God wants us to fall into His arms. He is ready and waiting to scoop us up and love us. We have to trust Him enough to let go and just float into His arms.

How do you gain child-like trust in God? By loving Him. Look at Him. Has He not proven His love that He died on the cross for us? Has He not said, while hanging on the cross, to the Heavenly Father, *"Forgive them, they know not what they do?" (Luke 23:34).* What love!

St. Therese offers herself to Jesus as a soul that can be consumed by His love! Wow! Can you believe that Jesus would honor such a request? He did for Saint Therese and He did for me too. He will for you as well.

Jesus is not loved like He should be because people often think that they have to be perfect before they approach Him. The reality is that you have to stay small and weak.

After I consecrated myself to Merciful Love, I was consumed by His love. When I would go in front of Him in Adoration of the Blessed Sacrament, He would just make my heart burn for Him. This didn't happen right away, but slowly as I let go of myself and became little, giving Him what love I had to offer, He took it with special care and gave me so much love that I could hardly contain myself sometimes. He just made my heart burn like the disciples on the way to Emmaus. *"Were not our hearts burning [within us] while he spoke to us on the way and opened the scriptures to us?" (Luke 24:32).*

Saint Faustina, whom I mentioned before, was the Apostle of Divine Mercy. The Lord also told her to become small so that He could do great wonders with her. She gave us the Feast of Divine Mercy along with the Divine Mercy Chaplet. I spoke of the power of the DMC when I shared our family praying it prior to Jon's surgery. Also, the beautiful image of Divine Mercy is a picture of Jesus dressed in a white tunic with two rays coming out of his heart, one red and the other white. These rays represent the blood and water which gushed out of his side when He was pierced by the lance on the cross. Can you imagine just getting touched by one drop of that water or blood? Just one drop of Jesus precious blood could heal a nation. Why, I wonder, do we not trust in Him? Jesus wanted the words "Jesus, I Trust in You" written on the bottom of the image. Jesus wants us to trust in Him. He wants us to give Him everything.

Before, I used to pray with my long laundry list of intentions and also the steps God needed to take to answer all of these intentions. I figured that I was helping Him since I knew better what was needed. Talk about pride.

Now, I say, "Jesus I trust in You. You take care of it." It is freeing to be able to just say that. I promise you that He will. His answers are always beyond your wildest dreams.

Even though I felt like I was making progress in my spiritual growth, I still had much work to do, but I didn't know how to do it and what was in the way.

# Chapter 13: Forgiveness

*Then Peter approaching asked him, 'Lord, if my brother sins against me,
how often must I forgive him? As many as seven times?' Jesus answered,
I say to you, not seven times but seventy-seven times.'*
*—Matthew 18:21–22*

I kept asking Jesus, "What is it that is keeping me from growing closer to You?"

My friend Susan helps with deliverance ministry at the Catholic church in a small town next to ours. Deliverance is dealing with the areas in your life where you have opened the door to Satan, most of the time, unintentionally. Sometimes it is by trauma; oftentimes it is unforgiveness.

There is a natural law that both God and the demons live by. Most people don't believe that the enemy exists these days. He definitely does. He wants to wound you so that you will never be happy. He wants you to fall into his traps so that you will disconnect from God.

Evil is real and when we open the door to it, we need to be delivered from it. Susan gave me the below steps to pray about and complete. She did mention to me that sometimes when you go through this that people are physically healed. I thought, *Well, maybe some small things like headaches or things like that, but this couldn't happen to me.*

Jon decided to go through these steps with me. They are:

Pray to the Holy Spirit to guide you to the people that you have to forgive and write it down on paper. I did this and it really helped me. I ripped it up and Jon burned his after we were done with it.

Don't forget yourself. You are the most important one! We think, for some reason, that we should never make mistakes in our lives. Boy, do we have some high expectations for ourselves!

If you are Catholic, go to Confession. If not, just say out loud from your heart to the Lord that you forgive your loved ones and others and yourself. You will be amazed at what happens afterward.

The key to this is that you have to try to love people the way God does: putting others before yourself, listening, not judging or trying to change them. The love must be unconditional.

It is hard when you think that God loves the serial rapist as much as the victims. His love isn't based on what we do; it is based on who we are. His children. Those of you who have rebellious children know, that even if you don't like what they do, even if it is really bad, like killing someone, you still love them and constantly hope and pray that they will change. This is exactly the way God feels, but He has a big family. All of us.

When I started to look at others as God's children and looked at all the wounds they had, I was able to forgive everyone. We are all wounded children and most of the wounds are due to our separation from God.

After this, I started to feel the presence of God within me. I would walk into church and just be overcome by the Holy Spirit. The love God has for us as His children is more profound than we can imagine. Just a taste of the love He has given me goes way beyond anything this world has to offer.

# CONFESSION

*"He who conceals sins prospers not, but he who confesses and forsakes them obtains mercy."*
—Proverbs 29:13

The Sacrament of Reconciliation (also known as Confession) drew me even closer to God's merciful love.

Reconciliation is confessing our sins to the priest who is acting as the person of Christ (in persona Christi). The first step is to confess our sins. Then we say an Act of Contrition, showing sorrow for our sins. The priest gives us some sort of penance, like prayers or something nice we can do for someone. Then we hear the words, "I absolve you of your sins in the name of the Father and the Son and the Holy Spirit." Those words are powerful.

Even though I attended Catholic school, I don't remember my family and I going to Confession on a regular basis. So as an adult, regularly celebrating Reconciliation was a foreign thought to me.

As I grew closer to God, I felt the sins on my soul, and I felt dirty. It's hard to describe. After I started to go to Confession monthly, I was more aware of the sins I committed. I felt unclean, but I also didn't know how to stop the same sins that I had been confessing for years. I wanted to change, but I didn't understand how.

I heard a talk from an exorcist priest, and he said that Confession was one of the most powerful weapons against the Devil. The Devil is the one who influences, tempts, and snares us into sin. Of course, we were born with concupiscence, an inclination to sin, which is why it is easy for us to get caught up in his snares.

This priest said that we receive such sanctifying grace from Confession that it breaks the Devil's hold on us. After I heard this, I decided to go to Confession more frequently. I would go every two weeks or sometimes weekly based on the condition of my soul.

What I noticed was that it was easier for me to stop those recurring sins. Of course, this is a lifetime battle, but I did notice a tremendous change in my attitude. I also try to have a keen awareness of what I say. My mouth gets me into a lot of trouble.

I started to work on the relationships within my family by practicing prudence, temperance, and fortitude. It wasn't easy, and it still isn't, but I knew this was the best place to begin. Jesus said to love our neighbors as ourselves, so I started to look at my family the way God looks at them.

I still fail miserably at it, but I am making progress.

# Chapter 14: Freed by His Love

*"How can I repay the Lord for all the great good done for me?"*
*—Psalm 116:12*

The year 2020 started off just like any other year. January was busy. I remember getting together with my children to celebrate a combined birthday dinner for everyone who had a birthday in January and February. My pain level started to get worse again. I didn't want to tell my family that even though being on my strict diet and supplements and going to my chiropractor, I was getting worse.

Despite all of this, I still went to church and sat with Jesus. It was time for Ash Wednesday and Lent to start. Lent is my favorite time of year. I love to offer up special sacrifices to the Lord. I always had pain to give to Him. I decided that this year, I would really offer up as much as I could to Jesus who suffered so much for me.

I have my list of my Lenten activities sitting right in front of me as I write this book. One of the bullet points is: Remember that I am a child. Another one is: Submit to God's will completely. Another one is: Read, *33 Days to Greater Glory.* This is the latest book by Father Michael Gaitley, which is a consecration to the Father through Jesus. The book concentrates on the Gospel of John, which I had read the month before. God had already prepared me. The Gospel of John is all about the love of Jesus and the Father. The whole story of Jesus and His Passion is a love story. The love of a mother who said "yes" to God and allowed her Son to go through this suffering. The love of the Father to beget the Son by the overshadowing of the Holy Spirit. The love of the Father who sacrifices His Son for our sake. The love of the Son who loves His Father (and us) so much that He allows Himself to go through the most brutal death imaginable.

Having a relationship with the Father was opened up to me a month before by Neal Lozano in his book, Unbound. He stated in the book that he didn't have a relationship with the Father and knew that there was something missing in his life.

In my walk with God, I knew that child-like trust was important, but I didn't think as much about the love of the Father for me. I contemplated my grandchildren, as I stated before, showing the child-like trust, but I didn't really understand that this trust comes with knowing that our Heavenly Father loves us. I knew that Jesus loved me, but I really didn't think about the love of God the Father. I was so excited to begin seeing my Heavenly Father as my father. When I am weak and small, my Heavenly Father would stoop down to me and scoop me up.

———————

March 6, 2020 will ever be engrained in my heart. I got up and went to Mass at nine a.m. at a Catholic church closer to my new home. Every Friday, they have Adoration of the Blessed Sacrament right after Mass until the evening. This was a special Friday as it was the First Friday of the month. I explained earlier that the First Friday of every month, there is special devotion to the Sacred Heart of Jesus.

I decided that I would stay awhile and brought my book, 33 Days to Greater Glory with me. I was reading along when I came to a page in the book where Father Gaitley talks about the paralyzed man who could never, in thirty-eight years, make it to the pool of water. I used to feel so sorry for him because I pictured people pushing him out of the way so he could never get close enough, which made him sad and lonely. I often related to him in this sense. But Father Gaitley had a different take on it. He said, "Maybe he's grown to love self-pity. Maybe he's allowed his handicap to define his whole identity."

When I read this, I looked at Jesus, and my heart sank. I said to Him, "Jesus, I hope that I am not comfortable with my illness. I know that I haven't asked You in a while, but You can heal me if You want to, but only if it is Your will and not mine." I had been so worried that I would go back to the person I used to be that I didn't trust Jesus to give me the grace to move forward. He wouldn't abandon me.

That evening, we were planning on going to this Parish Mission at a Catholic church far away from our home. Jon happened to be there for a men's conference the week before when the priest mentioned it. A priest who has the stigmata would be there.

For those that don't know what stigmata means, Jesus allows some people to participate in His Passion by actually bearing His wounds. Saint Francis of Assisi, St. Pio, and many others have had the wounds of Jesus.

My friend, Susan, told me that on every First Friday, the priest's, Father James Manjackal, stigmata bled. I was just so amazed because I had never had the experience of seeing someone in person who had the wounds of Jesus.

Father James was from India. He had a long white beard to match his white hair. His smile and love for Jesus was evident. He used a wheelchair due to the wounds on his feet. He had with him his long-time friend Gabby and her son Richi. Father James and Richi spoke about the Holy Spirit. Father James told of the amazing gifts of healing that God had given him.

At the end of the talks, Father James said that he would be praying over people. Both he and Richi first explained the laying on of hands as written in the Bible and how God had commissioned His disciples to go out and heal the sick and cast out demons.

My friend Mary and I had just been talking about the Holy Spirit and how we never really gave Him much thought. I felt the Holy Spirit had helped me to let go of the unforgiveness I had toward myself and the people who'd hurt me. After that experience, I was intrigued to learn more about the third person in the Trinity.

Jon and I brought our grandson, Riley. We wanted him to be prayed over because he had just gotten diagnosed with Type 1 Diabetes.

I prayed, "Jesus, can You please give my healing to Riley? He is young and has his whole life ahead of him." As I was continuing to pray before the laying on of hands started, I said, "Jesus, You are a big God, why am I minimizing what You can do? You can heal Riley and me if You want to. Whatever Your will is, I accept."

When it was time to walk up and receive healing, there was a long line in front of Father James. I was praying and keeping my eyes on the crucifix. From where I was standing, I could look over the people in line to the altar where the crucifix of Jesus was located. I just kept repeating to Jesus that if it is His will, He could heal me and Riley and that I trusted Him completely. I was going to wait in line for Father James, but I decided to go to Richi. Jon wanted me to go to Father James, and I said, "I am trusting in God. He is the healer and it doesn't matter who I go to."

When it was my turn, I told Richi that I had Trigeminal Neuralgia. He is a doctor so he understood. He asked me if it would be okay for him to lightly touch my face with his hand over the top of the face covering that I had on. I consented and he asked my name.

Richi's words were, "Jesus, Cheryle doesn't need this Trigeminal Neuralgia anymore. Jesus, I ask that You burn this away and take it to Your cross."

Within a second, I felt as if I was taken over by a strong force, like a strong breeze in the middle of summer. I could barely remain standing, swaying a little from the magnitude. It must be the Holy Spirit, but I never felt such a strong presence before in my life.

Every area that Richi was touching became hot, a burning sensation that was purifying. Within a blink of an eye, my pain was gone. It. Was. Gone!

I fell to the floor, crying and praising God. Riley got prayed over next. He was behind me in line. Jon came over to see what happened. I told him that I was healed. I took off my cover and for the first time in many years, I had no pain.

I just kept crying and saying, "I can't believe it. I have no pain." I had a full grin on my face again. Joy was overflowing. My heart was beating so fast and I just couldn't contain my joy. I wanted to run and tell the whole world. I walked by complete strangers and said that I was healed. I didn't care, and I still don't. I want everyone to know the love of God.

That night as we left the church, the wind was cold and strong. Jon, not quite grasping the fact that I was actually healed, wanted to go get the car. I said that I was walking right out the door. I walked in the wind. For the first time in such a long time, the wind was my friend again, the same wind that just a few hours ago caused me so much pain. Jon didn't know what to say. He was flabbergasted. Every bump we hit on the way home didn't bother me. I was calling all my girls. I texted my friend Mary and then I called her too. My children were crying and so excited on the phone.

When we got home, all of us, including my two daughters that we live next door to and my son-in-law were on our knees praying a rosary of thanksgiving for my healing.

The joy that I had was unbelievable. That night, I couldn't sleep. I just kept praising God for the amazing gift He had given His little girl. I remember waking up in the morning and feeling my face. No, it wasn't a dream, it had been real.

The next day I was contemplating about whether I should or shouldn't take my medication. For almost seven years, I was on the highest dose of Trileptal that a person could be on. I always tried to lower it some because it affected my eyesight.

By God's grace, the only place that I don't have double vision is my frontal vision. If I have to look up or down quickly, I just close my left eye. When I was on the highest dose, my eyes would all of sudden go double in my frontal vision. This happened one time when I was driving. I was so scared that I had to pull over.

I had fallen six times within the last year due to the high dose of my medication because it caused me to have an unsteady gait and dizziness. The worst fall was at home last year where I tore my right rotator cuff.

I texted Mary and asked her, "Do you think that I should continue taking my medication?" I knew the warning never to go off the medication without slowly reducing it over a period of weeks or months. Even if you never had a seizure before, coming down cold turkey could give you one. I'd never had a seizure but sure knew what they looked like.

Mary said, "I don't know. Ask Jesus." I prayed about it. I decided if Jesus healed me of all of this pain, I was going to continue trusting Him. I stopped taking my medication. As the days went on, I was waiting for any sort of withdrawal symptom to show up, but nothing. I had no withdrawals. Praise Jesus!

What I did notice right away from being off the medication is my eyesight got better. I still have double vision, but no blurriness. I have a strong gait. I no longer fall due to my unsteadiness and dizziness. I am able to think clearly with no brain fog.

My heart felt like it was going to explode from joy. I did cry a lot but they were tears of happiness. I felt so humbled. I am nobody special. I am a sinner just like you are. I don't know why God healed me. God's mercy is unfathomable.

On Saturday, I went back to the mission and my friend Mary and her husband were there. I ran up to her, with a big smile on my face, and we hugged and cried. Mary knew more about my trials than anyone else, other than family. She always prayed and helped me with a kind word here and there. I love her like a sister. I was blessed to have so many friends that always prayed for me.

I told Richi of my healing. He was not aware I'd been healed because I just fell to the floor in praise and thanks to Jesus. Richi had a huge grin on his face when I told him. He prayed over me again and touched my face in a very loving manner. He then prayed over my friend, Ofelia, that I brought with me, and he asked me to join him. He taught me the simple steps to pray, but he said the key is to have faith and trust. Both parties have to have faith and trust in God. He said that my grandson Riley has a healing, he just has to accept it. We are the obstacle of our healing when we don't have faith that God will actually heal us. He told me that oftentimes when Jesus heals someone, they continue to heal of other ailments.

I had neuropathy in my feet where I could not feel them from the ball of my foot to my toes. I can now feel my feet again. This happened within two weeks of my healing. I am also regaining feeling in my face and my head. Just two days ago, I was able to feel food on the left side of my lip. I was not able to smile fully because I didn't have control over my muscles on the left side due to the total numbness. (See appendix for pictures.)

## *SEEING IS BELIEVING*

I texted my friend Kim: "I was healed." But she didn't respond. I decided, on the spur of the moment when I was driving close to her house, to stop in. I walked to the front door and rang her doorbell.

Kim opened the door with eyes as big as saucers. Her mouth was open. She just stared at me in disbelief. "You look like the old Cheryle that I used to know." I told her, "No, I am the new and improved Cheryle." She told me when she got my text, she said, "Yeah right!" God wanted me to stop at her house to give her hope that He means what he promises. *"See how great a love the Father has bestowed on us, that we would be called children of God; and such we are. For this reason the world does not know us, because it did not know Him." (1 John 3:1).*

Running into friends and acquaintances, I often hear, "Cheryle, is that you?" "What happened?" "You look ten years younger." "You look radiant."

Already, I have spent endless hours playing outside with my grandchildren and a lot of time assisting in the planting and weeding of our family garden, canning the abundant produce. I went clothes shopping with my eleven-year-old granddaughter for the first time. She was too young to remember me healthy. I just cried thinking about it.

Just recently, I was called by the company that sells the electronic stimulator that my doctor wanted to implant in me. The sweet voice on the phone called to tell me that my insurance has now approved the payment of the stimulator. I just said, "Thanks, but I don't need it anymore. I have been healed." I proceeded to tell her my story. The lady on the phone was in tears. She said, "I am a Christian; can I tell your story?" I told her, "Please do! The glory is all God's. I didn't do a thing but just love Him." He asks for just a drop of love from us. In return, His love surpasses our wildest dreams.

Jon often turns to me and just smiles as I am dancing outside with my grandchildren. He is still in awe of God's wonder. His faith has grown tremendously. He tells me all the time that he can't get used to me just walking out the door. Every time I take a shower, I still cry. The other day it occurred to me that I can swim again! I used to swim all the time.

Jon and I drove over nine hours to visit Our Lady of the Angels monastery in Hanceville, Alabama in April of 2020 where Mother Angelica, the foundress of EWTN (Eternal World Television Network) lived with her cloistered nuns. Mind you, driving more than an hour used to be so painful for me. When we entered the monastery, I looked around at the familiar beauty of the main church. Every year before illness, Jon and I visited this monastery. EWTN has been a big part of our lives.

We often went to family gatherings that they'd have in Alabama before they started to have them in different states. I loved Mother Angelica because of many things, but her Italian heritage made me feel at home. Being full-blooded Italian myself, it was nice to know that God could actually take an Italian, like her and make her a saint (though not yet officially). This always gave me hope. My mouth is always the area I have trouble with. I speak before thinking.

Returning to the monastery was something I thought I would never be able to do. The mercy of God is so deep that we would never be able to physically see the bottom of the wellspring of love God has for us.

I just celebrated my one year anniversary since being healed. I still run into people who want to hear my story. I am a living miracle. My smile cannot be contained. I think and contemplate the love Jesus has for me. He healed me for some reason. I pray that I am able to live my life always remembering my healing. I want to never take anything for granted. I want to have faith to move mountains. I want to console Jesus' heart by loving Him. The refining fire still needs to keep burning within me. The same fire that healed me will continue to purify me.

I show Jon and the children more love and have spent so much time with my grandchildren. I laugh more, I love more, I don't put off for tomorrow what I can do for today. Most importantly, I give God my day and tell Him to use me in any way that He sees fit. I plan, but He takes over, and I try to accept with joy whatever He wants me to do for the day.

In one year, God has truly transformed my family's life. On Easter Vigil, my son-in-law, Matt will become Catholic along with his sister and niece. My daughter, Melissa, has moved only 8 minutes away from us and has returned to the Catholic church. On April 10th of 2021, her daughter, Ari will be making her First Communion. He has also blessed me with a new grandson yet to be born in May. God has answered so many of my prayers. I could never repay the Lord for all that He has done for me but I will spend the rest of my life trying. My love for Him surpasses any earthly desire. He has freed me.

I am free. Free of pain, free of worry, free of being in charge of my life. Instead, I let the Divine Healer take me where He wills. Like a child, I hold His hand and accept where He takes me. I have no fear. I trust in Him.

This is a favorite poem from an unknown author:

I know not what the future holds,

I only know that I am in God's hands,

I'll live and love, as life unfolds,

I'll trust Him, He understands.

JESUS, I TRUST IN YOU!

Jon and I the year before I was diagnosed.

After brain surgery.
I can't smile well due to numbness.

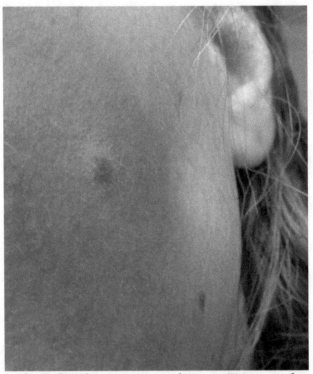

This is my face after the rainstorm when my Trigeminal returned.
It isn't common to actually see the pain a person is feeling with this
disease, but in this instance, it's apparent.

In this photo, you can see the weight I gained.
You can also see the pain in my eyes and my crooked smile.
Around my neck is the cover I would wear over my face.

Mary and I the day after my healing!

Me holding my grandchild.

Me playing outside with my grandchildren. Something I thought
that I would never be able to do.

As I celebrate my one year anniversary of my healing, I took this picture in front of the Holy Face of Jesus and Our Lady of Fatima pictures that I would gaze at tenderly when I couldn't get out of bed. Jesus and Mary, I love you.

CPSIA information can be obtained
at www.ICGtesting.com
Printed in the USA
JSHW080213101122
32909JS00006B/265

9 780578 809533